THE ELUSIVE TREASURE OF FORREST FENN

A Pursuit for More

Aaron Brown

ISBN-13: 9798666781494

Cover photo by: Eberhard Grossgasteiger

Scripture taken from the New King James Version. Copyright 1982 by Thomas Nelson.
Used by permission. All rights reserved.

Library of Congress Control Number: 2018675309
Printed in the United States of America

CONTENTS

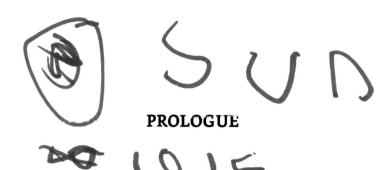

PROLOGUE

A n 800 year-old Romanesque chest was hidden some-where in the Rocky Mountains. The bronze chest is merely ten inches long by ten inches wide by five inches high, but its contents have enticed people from around the country. Gold, jewels, necklaces, bracelets, ancient rings, carved jade figures, and other surprises await the person who uncovers it.

Hundreds of thousands of people have searched with no luck, several dying in their pursuit. Each has felt confident in solving a poem's riddle, boasting the precise location of the treasure. And yet, none have stumbled upon the chest, discovering disappointment instead.

None of that would deter me, though. I was close. I could smell it.

I watched the helicopter rise, slowly turn away, and drift off until completely vanishing from sight. It would not return for forty-eight hours. "Oh...my...word. What did I just do?" I asked myself aloud. I could do that because I was alone. Perched high atop a mountain ridge, I was surrounded by grassland, forest, and steep cliffs. "I'm a moron," I assured myself. This was my first helicopter ride, an experience in itself, and the only reasonable manner for me to arrive at this Wyoming location. I lacked cell phone service, and there was no one around for miles.

I was beginning to stress out. The sun was hastily sinking, and I needed to set up a tent before the temperature suddenly dropped or a wild animal consumed me. Setting up a tent was a skill I had yet to attempt in my life. Why would I go camping, when hotels offer a pillow top mattress and comforter? But you would miss the outdoors, they say. That's where the flat screen comes into play, watching a movie like *The Revenant*, to witness a person getting mauled by a bear from the comfort of your temperature controlled room. But in the wilderness I presently remained, and feeling nervous was an understatement.

Scanning the area, my adrenaline quickened. I grabbed one of two bear repellant sprays from my amateur backpack. What if a bear suddenly appears and charges? What if a curious cub runs toward me? Surely the angry mama bear will be close behind to decapitate me. Perhaps a mountain lion will sneak up and pounce on my shoulders, claws tearing into back flesh as dagger-like teeth sink deep into my soft neck. How would I block a severed neck artery before my blood levels depleted? I would attempt fighting off the lion, of course, in which case it would behave frantically and maul me to shreds. If a venomous snake bites me, I am doomed. I would never get help in time. Too many horrific thoughts were attacking me at once.

DARK CAVE

T o understand how I ended up in this remote region of Wyoming, far from any semblance to humanity, I must back up a number of years.

My stepfather was a pastor throughout most of my childhood, so I went to church all the time. There was Sunday school, followed by Sunday church service, Wednesday night Bible study, and Friday prayer meeting at six o'clock in the morning. We had family devotions each morning around the breakfast table, where we read several chapters of the Bible, engaged in a time of prayer while holding hands, and attempted memorizing Scripture, before hurriedly rushing off to school. Now and then, we would visit a local nursing home where my dad would present a short message, we would sing songs with the attendees, and then recite verses. Afterward, we would wander around greeting the elderly with a handshake and a few words. Their hands were soft and boneless, and the women would pinch my cheeks and tell me how cute I was...not my butt cheeks, mind you, my facial cheeks, but it was horrifying nonetheless.

I was a goody goody, to say the least, throughout my high school and college years. After attending Moody Bible Institute in Chicago my freshman year of college, I transferred to Texas A&M University in College Station, Texas, to pursue a degree in business. Upon graduating in 1993, my brother and I opened a coffeehouse in the same town, named Sweet Eugene's.

It was then I became a womanizer. There were girls everywhere, I was single, and I had to make up for lost time. Don't worry, I still went to church every Sunday.

By the year 2000, I lost track of the number of girls I had been with. I also acquired a taste for day-trading in the stock market. The lure of earning great gains in a short time was all too tempting. The prior couple of years were proving exceptionally profitable in the market. Life was great.

Until the day it went horribly wrong. Browsing for positive press releases in order to day-trade the next stock, one article boldly stood out. A small tech company issued a press release that would propel its stock price immensely. I immediately sold all other stocks, and put everything into this one company. It was a sure win! And because of that, I decided to borrow all that I could and purchased a bunch more on margin. Four hours later, the closing market bell rang and I made a killing...on paper. I sold none of my shares, for few people had even seen this remarkable press release yet. The price would skyrocket in the coming days and weeks.

Due to rapid escalation in the stock price that day, the Security Exchange Commission quickly investigated, and what they discovered turned my life upside down. The press release was a lie, and the SEC promptly halted the further buying and selling of the company's stock. The president of the company was sentenced to eight years in prison, and I was in big trouble.

I lost everything...all of my prior gains, my entire savings, and an enormous amount of money on credit. To make matters worse, the IRS still demanded that I pay tax on all of the capital gains I had made in the market that year. Taxes in general are high, but the day-trader pays almost double. Any gains earned from stock trades bought and sold in less than a year are taxed at a much higher rate, and all of my gains had disappeared in an instant. Well, at least I can offset the earnings with my monstrous losses, I reasoned. Little did I know, if you *make* a load of money day-trading in the stock market, you owe a great deal of those capital earnings. But if you *lose* a great deal of money, you may only deduct three thousand dollars in losses per year! Panic set in like never before. It could take a lifetime—no, numerous lifetimes—to write those losses off!

Now owing a huge debt to the IRS, they were threatening to confiscate everything I owned. Bankruptcy was an option, but I determined instead to pay off every cent. I paid the IRS off completely in the coming months by placing all debts onto roughly fifteen credit cards. The government was off my back, but now credit card companies were charging high interest rates on the borrowed money.

I thought I was doing fine before this incident, until God slapped me around and yelled, "Enough!" I found myself in a dark cave with nowhere to turn. It was the worst time of my life—the *best* thing that ever happened to me. I always loved God in a shallow, impersonal way. He died for me. Nobody else had ever done that. But in my dire straits, it was then i fell *in love* with God.

THE CHALLENGE

I t was 1988. When Forrest Fenn was diagnosed with cancer at age 58, he decided he did not want to die a slow, miserable death. So he devised a plan. Gathering an array of valuables collected during his lifetime, he placed them in a chest, with the intention of dying alongside them. He would venture to a cherished and secluded area with the small trunk, swallow sleeping pills, and die. But he would leave behind a cryptic poem, leading the person who interprets it directly to the treasure. He survived the cancer, however, but retained his scheme of hiding the chest.

In 2010, when he was around 79 years old, he did exactly that. After spending 15 years formulating the poem to lead one fortunate soul to his enchanted place, he took a trek into the Rockies and hid his trove.

Fast forward to early 2018. I stumbled across a treasure hunt while surfing the web. I don't even recall how I happened upon it, but somehow it surfaced. The quest all hinged upon deciphering a poem that supposedly led the searcher directly to its location. I was intrigued, not so much in actually finding the treasure, but in merely cracking the interpretation of the poem. I wanted to solve it for the sake of solving it, nothing more. It was a challenge I could not pass up.

Forrest Fenn, the riddle's author, was clear that a person needed only the poem in order to discover the treasure chest he hid years prior. There were nine main clues throughout the poem, and I figured, I'm no genius, but I have just as good a chance in figuring it out as anyone else. I simply needed to think and solve the riddle. I love a good brainstorm.

The poem is comprised of six stanzas, each containing four lines, for a total of twenty-four lines:

> "As I have gone alone in there
> And with my treasures bold,
> I can keep my secret where,
> And hint of riches new and old.
>
> Begin it where warm waters halt
> And take it in the canyon down,
> Not far, but too far to walk.
> Put in below the home of Brown.
>
> From there it's no place for the meek,
> The end is ever drawing nigh;
> There'll be no paddle up your creek,
> Just heavy loads and water high.
>
> If you've been wise and found the blaze,
> Look quickly down, your quest to cease,
> But tarry scant with marvel gaze,
> Just take the chest and go in peace.
>
> So why is it that I must go
> And leave my trove for all to seek?
> The answers I already know,
> I've done it tired, and now I'm weak.
>
> So hear me all and listen good,
> Your effort will be worth the cold.
> If you are brave and in the wood
> I give you title to the gold."[1]

That was it. No huge words. It rhymed well enough. No big deal.

A few other details were offered by Forrest. The filled chest weighed around 42 pounds and was hidden in the Rocky Mountains, in one of four states, Montana, Wyoming, Colorado, or New Mexico. It was placed somewhere above 5000 feet and below 10,200 feet in elevation. And Mr. Fenn was abundantly explicit that it was at least 8.25 miles north of Santa Fe, New Mexico, his personal place of residence. So, no, it was not hidden in his home or on his property. Even so, someone used an ax to break into his home in 2018, hoping to discover the treasure inside. No, it was not me.

I soon had my very own solve for the poem. Studying Google Maps, I realized the chest was hidden in New Mexico, just north of Forrest Fenn's home in Santa Fe, and a smidge to the west. I began where a river of *warm waters halt* as it joined with a cooler river, and then I followed it down *too far to walk*. Just *below the home of Brown*, where an Indian reservation still exists, a dry creek curved away from the river. So far, so good. There would be *no paddle up your creek* since the creek was dry. A short distance away, I discovered the blaze, a giant white rock in the shape of a flame of fire. The chest should be directly below this rock. Wow, that was simple. And all from the comfort of my home computer!

Then I reasoned how boring the scenery of this place looked. Why would Forrest want to die in that spot? Why was that location so memorable to him? It didn't make sense. I must be mistaken.

I began reading poem solves of other searchers. Each believed his or hers to be correct, for each line of the poem could easily be justified by the scenic locale they ended up selecting. There was always a warm water source, it eventually halted at some point for some reason, there was an endless supply of canyons to fit the need, and some manner of a home of Brown could finally be mustered in each case. All solves had their own answers to heavy loads and water high, and a remarkable blaze of sorts materialized every time. But in the end, no one could ever seem to unveil the chest. Many searchers were so sure their solve was correct, they determined the quest was a hoax, for there was no treasure where they looked. Some grew angry.

Upon learning that over three hundred and fifty thousand people had physically gone searching, many of whom journeyed dozens of times, I pondered why this poem was so difficult to unravel. Forrest was adamant about understanding the initial clue of the poem, for without it, one would never find the chest. The remaining eight clues were useless unless you figured out the first. So obviously that was job number one. Nothing else mattered until solving the initial clue.

Forrest felt people were trying too hard to comprehend his poem. They were overly dissecting and analyzing it. He claimed the poem is difficult for many people since they think the clues are more complicated than they actually are. He also said it took him years to write the poem, tweaking it now and then, so each word was intentional. I figured, if this is true, then I should be alert to everything he says concerning the hunt, even beyond the confines of his poem.

The first clue is allegedly, "Begin it where warm waters halt." Most searchers were discussing the hot springs of the Rockies. I felt a subtle rebuke from Forrest when he affirmed few people were getting this initial clue correct, so it moved me to ponder an alternate meaning.

I have learned in my own experiences, that the majority is generally wrong. I say, generally, for sometimes the minority is, in fact, wrong. But be it politically, morally, judiciously, and so forth, I find the majority is typically mistaken. Even with movie reviews, I continually enjoy movies most critics do not, and I dislike movies that many praise. In the days of Noah, for those who trust the Bible, the majority was clearly in the wrong, as God found one sole man righteous. Only he and his immediate family were allowed to live. We may differ on this point, and that is okay. The majority will probably disagree with me, and that will further prove my point!

Anyway, I recall at some point, Forrest advising to think like a child when reading the poem. So I asked myself, I said, "Self, what would that line mean to you when you were ten years old?" When I was ten, I knew nothing about the hot springs of the Rocky Mountains, or even if there were hot springs there. So maybe it was referring to something else.

And then it dawned on me. At age ten, I certainly knew about evaporation. After a rain, the water warms beneath the rays of the sun, morphs to water vapor, and then rises, and rises, until the moisture at last halts, if you will, at cloud level to form clouds. Could there be some sort of cloud peak, cloud mountain, or cloud anything in the Rockies? Yes! There was both a Cloud Peak and a Cloud Wilderness, nearby one another in the Bighorn Mountains, in northern Wyoming. Interesting. Few people seemed to be searching in that direction.

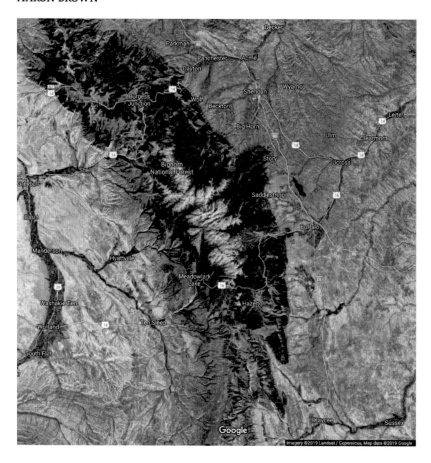

If this was correct, and "where warm waters halt," then I would need to "take it in the canyon down, not far, but too far to walk." And sure enough, there was a canyon headed south, for there seems to be a canyon heading south everywhere! I was not sold yet. I needed to find the home of Brown to continue in this vein of reasoning.

I had previously tried all manners of Brown, from brown bears, to brown homes, brown waters, brown trout, Brown Mountain, and people possessing the last name Brown (myself included). There were Browns all over the Rocky Mountains in one form or another. But at last, as I sought a southern path for thirty miles, I stumbled across a tiny Charlie Brown Spring. Now this took a while to find, for nothing stood out in the least, not even a spring. But it was not far, and clearly too far to walk, especially considering the rough terrain in arriving there.

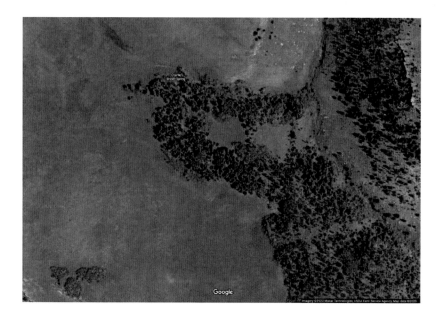

I struggled with this possibility for some time, for it truly appeared a rather insignificant landmark. Is this what Forrest Fenn was calling the home of Brown? It was obviously a name, so rightfully capitalized, but it was simply a small spring of water, and only during certain times of the year, apparently, for it looked utterly dry on the map. It seemed like a long shot.

I researched Charlie Brown, and learned that Charlie Brown, as a Peanuts character, made its official debut in 1950. Forrest was born in 1930, so he would have been about twenty years old at the time. Older people are nostalgic and tend to relish the olden days, the era from which they were raised. They always have, always will. This means Forrest grew up during the popular Charlie Brown cartoon era, and he probably finds the comic strip quite meaningful, even today.

As I continued reading, Charlie Brown was depicted as a nice, sweet, shy, and meek character.[2] Wait a minute! Meek? The next line in Fenn's poem reads, "From there it's no place for the meek." This could *not* be a coincidence! Or could it? The home of Charlie Brown was meek, but now the journey must grow more challenging.

The poem continues, "Put in below the home of Brown." Near the spring was a cliff, scaling about one thousand feet below, and a small river at its base. It appeared fairly shallow, so the "no paddle up your creek" made sense, and I assumed one should hike up river, so a paddle would be of no use anyway.

From there, I could figure nothing out. I felt the solve could possibly be correct, but the remainder of the poem was so incredibly vague. I read the poem over and over and over. And over and over again. I was stuck. Weeks went by. No other clues made sense. I recalled the words of Forrest. You need only the poem to find the chest, and maybe a good map, nothing more. Well, maybe a sandwich, but that's it. I remember thinking, "Yeah, that's all one technically needs. But Forrest knows where the chest is hidden, so of course it all makes sense to *him*! Nobody will ever unscramble this obscure, cryptic poem!"

I was frustrated. I should just give up. And I live in Texas, nowhere near the Rocky Mountains. What am I doing anyway? I'm an adult. I have a job. I have a family.

And I'm trying to find a hidden treasure chest? This is ridiculous, not to mention embarrassing if anyone finds out. Plus, the Rocky Mountains span over 10 trillion square feet, and I am supposed to locate a ten-inch box that may or may not be buried!

I seriously debated quitting. My thoughts wrestled within, as I sought sensible direction. Forrest claimed only he knew where the chest was hidden. He wisely concluded two people can keep a secret if one of them is dead. So not even his wife knew the location. A thought suddenly struck me. He is *not* the only one who knows where the treasure was placed! Someone else knows. *God knows.* Sounds corny, I'm with you. Well, it gets much cornier, trust me.

ALTERED PERCEPTION

I assure you this all pertains with how I unraveled the mystery of Forrest Fenn's hidden treasure. I would never have discovered what I believe was Forrest's special place without this chapter in my life, so bear with me.

God crushed me swiftly and painfully. Of course, I was humbled by the sudden mass of debt, no question. But my heart was broken and awakened by something vastly more critical. I found myself prostrate on the floor, my conscience condemning me of the life I was living. Never before did I comprehend the extent of God's love for sending his son to die for me.

I awoke to the depth of my depravity, and the height of God's holiness, an infinite gulf separating me from him. I recognized my desperate need to restore fellowship with God. I finally perceived the scope of what Jesus did for me; it became personal. He came to reside in a wicked world who hated him, and then die for that polluted world. He became hideous, repulsive, and cursed for *me*. Though sinless, he became at once every disgraceful act imaginable. Jesus became a womanizer on my account, he became a lover of money for my sake, and for every other shameful and disgraceful deed I ever committed, he assumed personal ownership.

No wonder God ceased walking with Adam and Eve in the Garden of Eden. It was not that he no longer desired to walk with man, but he no longer was *able*. Sin creates a proper chasm between that which is holy and that which is not.

Disgusted with myself, I repented and submitted to Christ. Not a joyful, high-five conversion, but one alone and sobbing. I began learning and appropriating the fear of God as he always intended. I yielded everything over to him, tangible and non-tangible. It proved gut-wrenching, but he was all that mattered now.

I still had debt...lots of it. The clouds did not scroll back for the sun to shine rays of splendor upon me. I still had tough times. But I changed that day. I was a different person, for my perspective and life purpose transformed. Temptations continued to pursue me, but my ambitions were amended. I began electing to turn *from* sin. Sin no longer controlled me, and for once, I set out to please God.

I remember praying one day for God to give me a desire to read his Word. Within a couple of days, I honestly began hungering for it. I looked forward to pouring into it. This boring, antiquated book was now alive! God's promises were applicable to *me* today, as were they when initially penned, if only I *first* met the conditions. What hope filled my soul, for my fate truly hinged upon my behavior. Every choice I make, whether to obey or evade God, would condition the remainder of my life.

Suddenly, I could not wait to get off work, so I could return home and study. The Old Testament was my personal story. The Israelites fell into sin, God punished them, and they repented and sought God. God would promptly forgive and move to bless them. Shortly after, the people of Israel would turn from God and behave wickedly. Harsh consequences would befall, they would repent, and God would mercifully forgive and restore them once more. Sin, discipline, repent, and blessing. Over and over, God lovingly chastised his people, in order to draw them back to himself, and shower them with his favor.

People are forever asking why bad things happen, and if there really is a loving God. Unfavorable events occur *because* he is a loving God. God has graciously awarded man free will. Bad things often transpire because immoral people behave wickedly. But He is holy, so a consequence for evil must ensue. Rebelling against God removes his protection and welcomes adverse consequences. Other times, unfavorable things occur in attempt to move us closer to him. How swiftly most of us would drift from God if we possessed everything we ever wanted. Our perceived need for God would rapidly diminish.

A better line of questioning may be as to why God allows us to continue living, as we persistently rebel against his ways. And how fair is it that he appointed his son to die for the corruption in the world? I am thankful he is not fair in that regard, but indescribably gracious.

I learned that pleasing God prompted the favor of God, and on the contrary, disobeying God assured a curse. This principle is reinforced in Scripture time and time again, almost to the point of exhaustion. *Now, gaining God's favor in no way guarantees a life of wealth and health.* The opposite may occur, but we remain in his favor nonetheless, and it is God who decides whether to bless now or later. But living to please God inspired me, and that was sufficient enough.

I discovered embracing Jesus and honoring God opened the ears of God. Scripture is clear that God closes his ear to the sinner, but there is power in prayer for the righteous. Not perfect, mind you, for none are righteous apart from the work Jesus completed upon the cross. So I determined to fear God, turn from sin, and gain his favor, come what may.

Fear God and gain his favor, or else shun God and be cursed. I noticed few people truly fear God. Compromise is everywhere and commonplace, even within the Church. The Bible claims, "For the eyes of the Lord run to and fro throughout the whole earth, to show Himself strong on behalf of those whose heart is loyal to Him" (2 Chronicles 16:9).

I was excited about being different, about standing out in the eyes of God. Call me greedy, call me selfish, but I wanted God to notice *me*! I wanted the intimacy with God he promises. This single principle was an aha moment for me, inflaming a fresh perspective in my life.

THE ORACLE

I must back up once more. I was so annoyed and weary of prosperity messages, that in 2016, I was burdened to write one myself, entitled *THE ORACLE: Universal Law of Prosperity Defying All Others.* It goes against all man-fabricated prosperity messages, as well as gospel messages guaranteeing prosperity. Instead, it reveals a profound, yet simple principle I learned from studying God's Word. It embraces the universal divine law, whereby a person gains the favor of God upon his decision to fear him. By fearing the Lord, a person chooses to simultaneously turn *toward* God, and *away* from sin. One may do so from fear of negative consequence, or hopefully the loftier reason of loving God so much, he desires to obey him, shunning sinful behavior.

Hundreds and hundreds of verses support this principle, from Genesis to Revelation, but they likewise come with a severe warning. The individual, or nation for that matter, who does *not* fear God, but instead runs toward a lifestyle of sin, will not be blessed, but rather cursed. Deuteronomy 28 specifically outlines the numerous blessings for obedience and curses for disobedience. It is worth the read if you have never done so, for the promises of God are as alive and active today as they were when initially written.[3]

Now before anyone starts freaking out, I make it clear in *THE ORACLE* that choosing obedience to God's manner of living does *not* guarantee one will become financially wealthy, enjoy impeccable health, and so forth. Sometimes a wicked person grows in riches while a godly individual dies penniless. An evil man lives to one hundred, while a righteous man dies at age twenty. Nonetheless, the godly person still lives in God's favor, though God may choose to take his life prematurely. So, while it is indeed a prosperity message, it is unlike others in that the promises are penned by God, not man. They are *divine* promises, not superstitious fabrications of man.

I felt confident the premise for my book would be unpopular with those who believe not in the Bible. That was a given. But I was amazed by the number of Christians unmoved by the blessings promised. Surely a biblical message promoting the favor of God and one that opposes all counterfeit prosperity messages would be warmly welcomed, I reasoned. Upon noticing the book, a friend of mine inquired what it was about. I explained it in a few short sentences, and he literally laughed out loud. "You actually believe that?" he asked, laughing enthusiastically. "Yes, I trust God's Word," I replied. The subject promptly changed.

Satan is cunning. Due to the plethora of man-inspired prosperity messages today, the Christian is tempted to dismiss the God-inspired message of prosperity. Many of these believe the Christian should be persecuted and experience continual hardship, rather than blessing. We should carry our cross, so to speak. And while it is true, the Christian must be willing to carry any cross, any burden God sends his way, standing ready for inevitable persecution, this gives him no grounds to water down God's promises to a state of emptiness and lukewarmness. Ironically, I find few people living in hardship who profess the life of hardship we should encounter. In fact, I see many of these building grander homes, buying finer cars, and vacationing extravagantly.

God wants to bless those who fear and follow him. Even now, he desires to bless his chosen people, Israel, if only they would repent and turn back to him. Sadly, he withholds much favor as they firmly reject his Son whose blood for them was shed.

It saddens me to witness this lack of belief in the Word of God, and the promises God offers if only we first meet the conditions set forth. I was overwhelmed with a burden of guilt for the Church, myself included, for our lack of trust and obedience toward God. And I'll be honest, I was a bit bitter toward those who belittled and rejected the premise of *THE ORACLE*. I took careful measures to neither manipulate Scripture with thwarted slant, nor borrow verses beyond context, and I definitely did not write for selfish gain. In fact, for the first three years offering the book for sale in our cafe, I lost only one dollar for every book sold! I simply wanted people to read it and personally embrace God's promises he generously extends to each of us.

And yet, a lack of faith in God's promises and foundation for my writing was clearly evident. I finally realized, I can't take it personally, for those who scorn God's promises were not rejecting me, but God.

I confessed to God my bitterness, and politely informed him that it is *his* problem, not mine. It's *you* they don't believe! I repented of my resentment toward others, and allowed his promises to stand on their own accord, for they endure true and applicable whether one trusts in them or not. Not that God required my allowance, but rather I needed to free myself of the outcome.

A beautiful thing occurs when a person genuinely

repents. God immediately listens and forgives. God is clear, the unrepentant soul need not bother praying, for he will not be heard. But the humble he hears with open ears. No wonder most prayers seem to go unanswered.

So at the brink of giving up on the treasure hunt, my interest in it suddenly changed. Recognizing God knew precisely where the chest was hidden, I decided to ask for his direction. I prayed for God to reveal to me the mysteries of Forrest's poem. God had all wisdom and understanding, and nothing is done in secret, so I was confident he could do so. By this point, I was convinced it would not be me who deciphered the riddles, so I promised God I would give him all credit and glory. What I did *not* tell God, however, is that I would give all the money to charity once found. That is a classic rookie mistake, because then I would have to give it all away! I jest, of course. Sort of. No, I'm totally kidding. Sort of.

Fenn's poem is written in cryptic fashion, wielding double meanings and word plays to extract the essence of his intended meaning. While not the same, it nevertheless reminds me of Jesus speaking in parables, illustrating the unfamiliar spiritual realm with familiar concepts from the physical realm. When he spoke about sheep, Jesus referenced those people following him, as sheep are known to pursue their shepherd. Teaching on the kingdom of God, he employed farming terminology referencing farmers, seeds, chaff, vines, fruit, and various types of soil. He taught in this manner so those with spiritual discernment would understand, while those unbelieving and unwilling to receive him could not.

The Bible, in a way, is similar. While an unbeliever finds it difficult to comprehend the Word of God, the believer mysteriously gains insight. God is generous to the soul in pursuit of him, eager to open the eyes with knowledge and spiritual understanding. "But the natural man does not receive the things of the Spirit of God, for they are foolishness to him; nor can he know them, because they are spiritually discerned" (1 Corinthians 2:14).

Anyway, I recall when God revealed to Daniel the interpretation of the King of Babylon's dreams. I told God I lack understanding, and I give up on the poem. If I am to interpret it and discover the treasure, it would *only* be because of him, not me.

Now this will be difficult for most to believe, but I prayed for this unselfishly. In fact, this was one of the most unselfish prayers I have ever petitioned. I am embarrassed to admit, many of my prayers are selfish in nature, no question. But this one was entirely different. I was burdened to tears, quite literally, shameful in the lack of trust in God and his Word by his own followers. A heavy anguish filled my heart and an anger toward man's (including my own) lack of reverence for God and his Word filled my soul. Quite rare, admittedly, but I have shed tears in prayers before, but these were generally tears for God to deliver me from a personal trial or painful experience. These tears, however, emanated from the world's profaning of God's revered name.

I asked God to grant me understanding and unveil the treasure's location for the sake of validating his promises and his Word. Not for my sake, for I so believe in his promises that I wrote a book hoping to convince people in their relevance. Instead, *I wanted validation so others might believe.* This may be hard to accept, but it was not a prayer for me to find gold or gain money. It was a petition for God to receive glory, for his Word to be revered, in the hope that some would believe. I told you it would sound corny, but there you have it.

Now granted, my prayer included finding the gold, but again, that was not the end in itself, simply the means to an end (that some would believe). Had there been no treasure, or merely fifty dollars hidden, I would not have petitioned God to reveal it. Why? Because fifty dollars is not much money. Then it *was* about the money, you say! No, for no one would have cared were it but fifty dollars. Raise the stakes, however, and interest rises proportionally. So, in a way, I prayed for wisdom *because* of the money, but *not* because of the money.

The next day, I read the poem again and something tugged at me. "So why is it that I must go and leave my trove for all to seek?" Forrest claimed every word was intentional. The "why" could refer to Wyoming. The slogan for the state of Wyoming is "That's WY," so that could easily be meaningful.

Furthermore, once you put in below the Charlie Brown Spring, the poem affirms, "the end is ever drawing nigh." So, obviously you are close. I believe Forrest said you could walk to the chest from the home of Brown. If you follow the North Fork Powder River, directly below the Charlie Brown Spring, and travel west, or upstream about one mile, you arrive at a large "Y", sort of sliced out of the mountain ridge. Maybe that is what he is referring to. And if you altered the question into a statement, it would read, "So why is it that I must go," or "So Y is it that I must go." Perhaps I need to go into the Y, I reasoned. I was not sold, but it conformed well enough.

Wait. Was that an answer to prayer? I wanted to believe so. I hoped so. Again, I was burdened to pray for God to receive glory in revealing more of the poem to me, that others might believe.

I am pretty sure it was the next day that another piece of the poem sprung to life. "Just take the chest and go in peace." I always felt this must mean more than the obvious. It finally occurred to me I needed to go in *peace*! The giant Y carved amidst the mountain range sort of resembled a peace sign minus the circle around it. And then I considered, when you offer someone the peace sign with your fingers, it also resembles a Y. That's it! Or was it? I still was not convinced, though glad to make the connection. I thanked God for the revelations, for I knew I would not have seen these things had I not asked.

I attended church that Sunday, three days after my initial prayer for God to validate his promises. I do not recall presently on what the pastor spoke, but in the middle of the message, he said he wanted to see God work miracles. He immediately clarified he did not want to see them for the sake of seeing miracles, but for the sake of *validation*. What the what! I perked up. I know, I know... coincidence.

I continued to pray for guidance. Only Forrest and God knew where to go. "Just heavy loads and water high." Studying a map further, I saw a tiny, dry creek atop the mountain ridge directly above and beyond the Y, that actually trickled down *into* the Y when water overflowed from a small nearby pond. Could this be the "water high" referred to in the poem? Seemed plausible.

If you follow the North Fork Powder River upstream several miles from the Y, it led to a larger reserve of water, the Dull Knife Reservoir. Water runoff from area mountains formed a quaint river that fed into this reservoir. A huge dam contained the body of water on the east side, with water flowing from the dam's base when full. It was this water flow that developed the North Fork Powder River, leading to the Y in question. That could definitely be the "heavy loads and water high," with the dam impeding heavy loads of water.

Forrest mentioned the chest will be wet, in some manner anyway. I could envision that now. He claimed he walked less than a few miles to hide the chest, two trips from his car and back. The distance to the Y fit. In one interview, he advised bringing "a flashlight and a sandwich." While a cave it was not, the Y did appear fairly deep, allowing less sunlight down into the crevice. Forrest mentioned on several occasions that one key word in the poem would help more than the others. I now believe that key word is *why.* My solve was taking shape.

BREAKTHROUGH

E very once in a while, I enjoy a season of compelling prayer. I say enjoy, but realistically, it is more of an anguish of soul, a wrestling of mind and conscience with the Spirit of God. More often than not, however, I feel my prayers lack effectiveness and power, undoubtedly due to my self-absorbed requests, or lack of close fellowship with God at the time. But then there are occasions when my heart and desires align with those of God, and an unrelenting urgency prods me to pray. It is this spirit of prayer I have grown to thirst for, a deep longing and desperation for something I believe God prompts us to petition, sometimes persistently, and other times simply for the moment.

Years prior, at eighteen months, our youngest daughter was unexpectedly diagnosed with hemolytic uremic syndrome (HUS), a condition involving the destruction of red blood cells and platelets. These damaged cells may then obstruct the kidneys, and possibly lead to kidney failure. She was admitted into the Texas Children's Hospital in Houston for two weeks, where my wife remained relentlessly by her side.

Burdened to be alone one evening, I slipped outside the hospital and began walking down the quiet streets of the enormous medical district to seek God's presence. Turbulent times have a way of provoking a person to pursue the profound, a deeper significance beyond their personal realm of current circumstance.

It was around 10 o'clock, and I noticed few cars at all on the roads, and even fewer pedestrians. While people fought for their lives within the surrounding hospitals of the medical district, a peaceful serenity endured outside. God was tugging at my heart, as I wrestled with areas of my life from him withheld. I knew God did not care about religion. He was not impressed with my church attendance, unmoved by my tithing, and to an extent, indifferent in my moral behavior. What he desired was my heart...*all of it.* My present adversity awakened my need to get right with God.

Strolling along, I softly prayed, yielding all that I have and all that I am. My possessions, my job, my loved ones, they were all his to either bless or to take. I repented of past sins, I repented of present sins. I was weary of the weight of guilt associated with my offenses. I wanted to live differently, to be uniquely his, without wavering or compromise. I wanted to live for God, to obey and please him, no matter what.

I prayed for many blocks, tears welling up. I finally concluded my repentance and surrender to God, and few will believe, I am certain, but a wind immediately burst forth on the street the precise moment I ceased praying... literally, that second. Where there was no wind along my stroll before, it suddenly blew at 35-40 miles per hour. The only other three pedestrians on the street bolted for the closest building, one shrieking aloud because of the sudden surge of wind.

It seems odd now, I admit, but I simply continued walking, with effort and strain, but with an overwhelming sense of peace and calmness. This occurred in the middle of a block, in case one imagines it at an intersection, where perhaps a little wind might pick up in the absence of buildings. Thirty seconds after it began, the wind suddenly died completely, just as quickly as it began. I turned around at the end of the block to return to the hospital, and there was no wind the entire walk back. When once a person surrenders his life, not simply in word, but in truth and sincerity, the Spirit of God is capable of more fully indwelling a soul. A complete yielding of the mind and will is mandatory.

Eccentric? I would not belittle the sentiment. People have always viewed those with unusual notions and experiences as eccentric. I hear someone now, "He thinks his prayer was answered. That's cute. Good for him." Skeptical? I don't blame you. The world is full of charlatans, and a measure of skepticism is generally warranted.

But God is alive and active, and he is present to the one who genuinely surrenders. Regrettably, as I witness answers to prayer, I rarely tell anyone, for I am certain they shall fall upon deaf ears. I am convinced a divine encounter typically amounts to little except to the one intimately involved. While the faith of a person affected flourishes, the one untouched, for the most part, remains mundanely uninspired. I believe God intentionally deepens faith in that fashion.

I continue to praise God for healing our daughter during that trial, and for protecting her from kidney damage or other complications. There is power in effective prayer, but before I wander too far, I shall resume.

And so, the more I prayed, the more clues were brought to light, each often the day after spending time in prayer. One line of the poem reads, "So hear me all and listen good." I envision walking into the deep, narrow crevice of the Y, with steep rock cliffs towering on each side of me. I imagine speaking, and the amazing echo and acoustics all

AARON BROWN

around. Could this be what he meant? Maybe, maybe not, but something to keep in mind. Perhaps it was a reference to a *horn*, alluding to the Bighorn Mountains. The following line claims, "Your effort will be worth the cold." The area map shows amazingly few roads in the vicinity, some barely grassy ranch roads or dirt paths. Possibly the nearest, more durable road, shimmied just to the east of this property and was named, Mayo-*worth* Road. Was this the route Forrest took to reach his destination? Again, not a grand epiphany, but another circumstantial suggestion. Perhaps it was necessary to cross through the chilly river once or twice to arrive at the destination.

I pondered the third line of the poem, "I can keep my secret where." Not only was this difficult to interpret, it neither seemed pleasing to the ears or flow fluidly within the context of the lines before and after. And yet, as Forrest confirmed, every word is intentional. The *where* seemed an odd choice of word to choose. There had to be a reason for selecting it. The only thing I could muster was a connection with the North Fork Powder River I would need to trail upstream. A fork is certainly a type of *ware*, as in silverware. I jotted the idea down, but nothing earth-shattering by any means.

A couple of days later, I was sure I had a breakthrough. I needed a crystal clear clue to support all of the small, potential coincidences. The fifth stanza reads:

"So why is it that I must go
And leave my trove for all to seek?
The answers I already know,
I've done it tired, and now I'm weak."

The wording in the last line of this stanza intrigued

me. The obvious meaning is, of course, implying that Forrest is older now, he carried the heavy treasure to the hiding spot, and now he is tired and weak. But there had to be more, there must be a double meaning, or he could have simply left this entire stanza out. But he did not. And so it bothered me.

Okay, you guessed it. I asked God for help. And then I saw it. Directly north of the Y, in fact, so directly north it was feeding *into* the Y. A peculiar body of hundreds of trees were growing amidst a prairie, and together they formed an unmistakable number *seven*...not the word seven, but the number 7. The configuration was too precise to deny! Maybe that is what Forrest meant by the word *weak*. Seven days comprise a week, and he altered the spelling by one letter, along with the double meaning. This new revelation seemed clever, but was I reading into something not there? Was I merely formulating my solve to fit my need for an answer?

I pressed on, examining the layout of the land. Oh. My. Goodness. You have to be kidding. How did I not see this sooner? To the immediate west of the number 7 tree formation was approximately 500 feet of prairie land. Promptly to the west of this open grassy space was another tree pattern, consisting again of hundreds of green trees. The cumulative design these trees composed proved just as unique as the 7 arrangement. It embodied a giant circle of trees, the diameter of which perfectly matched the number 7 in size.

So what? Well, the center of the tree circle was nothing but grass, forming an enormous number zero, again perfectly matching the size of the 7 to its right. So the two tree clusters together appeared from an aerial view as 07. At first, the zero did not resonate with me. But a lightbulb flickered. It's not a zero. It's a *tire*! "I've done it *tired*, and now I'm *weak*." Forrest could have easily said it the other way around, "I've done it weak, and now I'm tired." But that would have been 70, the improper way in which the trees were aligned.

I again gave thanks to God.

THE BLAZE

I needed more. On a beautiful day with white billowy clouds, if I want to see an elephant in the sky, I will discover a cloud that looks like an elephant. If I am looking for a dragon, suddenly a dragon-shaped cloud appears. Am I finding signs simply because I am searching for those specific signs? If I am going to travel to Wyoming, I had to be certain.

I scoured the internet for possible hints from Forrest Fenn himself. Fenn thought his clues could remain the next hundred years, but felt the geography would change over the course of a thousand. If the chest was hidden somewhere in the Y, the steep, rocky crevices could very possibly erode or crumble apart in that duration of time.

I still lacked any likeness of a blaze. Searchers speculated a wide plethora of ideas for the blaze, with little certainty. A few suggestions included large rocks, waterfalls, and markings on trees. What could it be and would I be able to identify it from my home computer? I prayed again for God to reveal this mystery. I knew he could, and if he were unwilling, I would still give thanks, for I do not deserve to find the chest anyway. But if it did align with his will, or was not contrary to it rather, I prayed he would be pleased to do so.

Within a day or so, my answer came. I studied the various meanings of blaze. It could mean a burning fire, a bright light, a burst of color, to fire a gun repeatedly, or to achieve something great. Then I somehow stumbled across the blaze of a horse. What? Sure enough, a horse blaze is generally a white marking between the forehead and nose of the horse. Every marking is unique in size and shape for each horse, much like a human fingerprint. I never realized this, but when a horse owner registers his horse, oftentimes the blaze on its face will be recorded to identify the rightful owner.

I ran across an old black and white photo that I am pretty sure depicts Forrest Fenn sitting atop a beautiful horse with a small white blaze on its forehead. The photo was from one of his books featuring him in his early days. No way. Could it be? I quickly checked the Y on the map. There it was. The immense rock jutting into the central point of the Y embodied the blaze! It dissected the two upper branches of the Y. Both blazes, from the horse and the rock, even resembled an arrowhead! I was shocked. I recalled my prayer, and paused to give thanks.

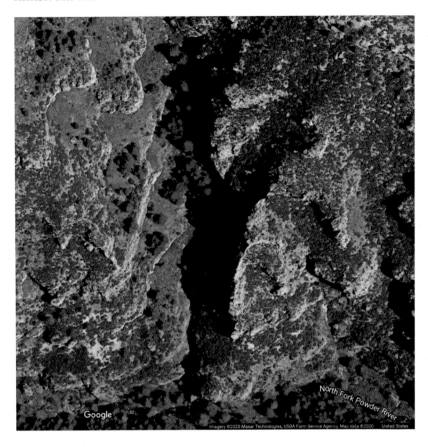

Was this blaze congruent with everything we knew? From emails Forrest constantly receives, he claimed some searchers had been within 200 feet of the chest. They walked right past the blaze, but never recognized it. This to me was now justifiable. If searchers were on the ground and hiking along the river, they would certainly miss the blaze entirely, for it stood hundreds of feet above ground level, and only visible from overhead. One could easily meander past it without knowing, and thereby pass right by the Y. The 200 feet might measure the distance from the river to the inner Y where the chest was potentially hidden.

Another hint within the line, "If you've been wise and found the blaze," could possibly be the word *wise*. Since the blaze was only detectable from high up in the air, maybe it implies an owl. Owls are known to be wise, for whatever reason I know not, nor do I care to google the logic, but wise they must be, especially if they are able to spot the blaze from above!

I felt secure in my new blaze. Searchers assumed all sorts of ideas for the blaze, with numerous posing questions to Forrest Fenn himself. I recall one inquiring which direction the blaze faced—north, south, east, or west? Fenn's response strengthened my new blaze even more, replying he did not believe it faced any of the four directions. A brilliant answer, for if the blaze was indeed what I believed, it did, in fact, face none of those directions.

It was then I contemplated dimensional space. Maps generally portray a two-dimensional field of scope, where one visualizes a distinct north, south, east, and west. Even with a three-dimensional map, one might simply assume those same dimensional directions. But there are obviously two additional directions—up and down. My blaze clearly faced upward, thus justifying Fenn's reply, and solidifying the notion of a searcher walking past it without noticing.

Other pieces to the puzzle began to fit. The chest was said to be hidden nowhere near a human trail. There were definitely no roads or paths in this area that I could detect.

Studying the line, "The end is ever drawing nigh," another subtle possibility surfaced. The word *draw* may elude to another meaning entirely. In geology, when used as a noun, a *draw* is "a gully shallower than a ravine."[4] A *gully* is "a trench which was originally worn in the earth by running water and through which water often runs after rains."[5] And a *ravine* may be portrayed as "a small narrow steep-sided valley that is larger than a gully and smaller than a canyon and that is usually worn by running water."[6]

The double meaning of the word *draw* harmonized perfectly. The Y carved within the mountainside was undoubtedly formed from years and years of running water, creating a narrow trench in the earth. A steep, double-sided valley was thus born, constructing the large Y in question.

I have always viewed myself as an optimistic realist. In certain situations, some might call me a pessimist, but I have grown to assume a degree of adversity in much of reality. Events often develop contrary to the way we anticipate. That's life. So even when something looks good and feels right, I tend to err on the side of caution.

That said, I felt eighty percent confident in my solve of the poem. My lovely wife, Andrea, was nowhere near as convinced as I, but she believed in *me*. I am not exactly sure what that means, except she was willing to accompany me wherever I believed we should go in life. Is that not the point of marriage, to now live as one flesh, sacrificing for the other when necessary? Attain a spouse like this. A suitable spouse will prove a treasure worth more than much gold.

So, we are moving to Wyoming! Okay, maybe not moving. We are traveling to Wyoming!

FIRST TRIP

W e flew into Casper, Wyoming, late June 2018, rented a car, and drove north toward the town of Buffalo. Wide open prairie land and rolling hills abounded. Where was everyone? The highway was unlike any we had driven in Texas. We could drive for miles without seeing another car. Life was different here. I always knew Texans were friendly, compared to much of the country, but the residents of Wyoming seemed even friendlier. Everyone smiled and most extended a warm greeting before we had a chance to offer one. We stepped back in time. The state enjoyed a small town feel, and life was unhurried and calm. There was so much lonely land, so much wild west still available to explore.

After buying supplies, my wife and I drove around forever. You see, we knew this would be a challenging trip, for an enormous problem awaited us. The chest, we believed, was hidden on an area of public land *surrounded by private land*. Completely. Surrounded...by private land!

We prepared as best we thought. I printed a map showing all public roads, which were sparse, to say the least. Many of these included ranch roads, which were hardly roads at all, but simply dead grass paths created by an occasional pickup truck driving through a field. But internet sites assured me these remained public paths on private land, for emergency vehicles needed access in case of fire, accident, or other predicament.

Wrong! Wrong! Wrong!

We drove around and around this immense private area of land the entire day. All gates were locked, some double-locked. Those were not public paths at all. We saw little signs of life anywhere, except for the occasional wild animal. Wild sheep roamed the hills. A type of deer lurked about in the grasslands...not white-tail, mule, or antelope. It was brown, had antlers, four legs, and looked savory, that's all I know. A possible eagle perched upon a nearby fence. Yes, I say possible, for it was bigger than a bread box, larger than two bread boxes. I could be mistaken, though, for I've never seen an actual bread box.

The trip proved disheartening. We made it within five miles of our destination, but we were unable to advance any closer. I tried contacting landowners, in person, via phone, even snail mail, in hopes of receiving permission to cross their property in order to reach the public land. No luck. They possessed a monopoly on the public land. Nobody had access but the private landowners. They controlled thousands of acres of public land all for themselves. The public river was all theirs. The public fishing, all theirs. The public hunting, theirs. Public camping, climbing, exploring...theirs, theirs, theirs!

I am reminded of the line, "Your effort will be worth the cold." It clearly will take *effort* to maneuver past the private land to arrive on public ground. Maybe *cold* referred to the surrounding landowners who proved unhelpful and unfriendly, as opposed to warm and hospitable. I suspect this was one of the reasons Forrest hid the chest where he did. Forrest loved to explore and fish, and I imagine he felt cheated in not being allowed to do so on more than 10,000 acres of public land, especially an area with historical Indian significance. Fenn was an avid collector of Indian relics and artifacts.

This begged a crucial question. Fenn claims he took two trips by foot from his parked car to the chest site in one afternoon...from car to site, back to car, and again from car to site, and back to car. He pulled this off at 79 years old while carrying a heavy weight of gold...not to mention, a sandwich. What type of sandwich, we know not. But to pull this off, Fenn would have needed to park his sedan fairly close. This was the dilemma that wrestled my confidence in the solve.

Was he able to drive in closely years prior than we were able today? I learned that one large landowner (in quantity of acres, not in human size) who bordered the public land was born four months before Forrest Fenn. Perhaps they were friends, and Forrest was allowed land access years prior.

Another thought hit me. What if Fenn's sedan was actually a helicopter, granting him easy entry into the barricaded public land? After all, he *is* a helicopter pilot. A sedan can be defined as possessing a three-part configuration with separate compartments for cargo, engine, and passenger, similar to helicopters. It can also depict a motorboat, or even a covered chair designed to transport a person by means of poles.[7]

Even though I know what a car is, I determined to probe further. A car may be described as an automobile on wheels, like a chariot or railroad vehicle. It may refer to an elevator compartment. Or, it might represent "the part of an airship or balloon that carries the passengers and cargo."[8]

A car can be part of an *airship*? I had to look it up. An *airship* is "a lighter-than-air aircraft having propulsion and steering systems."[9] An example given portrayed German airplanes carrying bombs across the seas during World

War I.

I researched further still, and found a beautiful connection. The rotastat is a type of hybrid airship employing rotary wings or blades for heavy lifting, even while hovering in the air, such as a helicopter.[10] I was delighted to discover the alliance between a car, a sedan, and a helicopter! Forrest Fenn relishes in manipulating words with multiple meanings for personal intention. He becomes designer and creator of cryptic word associations that puzzle and perplex by ever so gently tweaking words to his persuasion.

Reminiscing on past photos and quotes from Forrest, he seems to have a curious admiration, if not fascination, for dragonflies and hummingbirds. Dragonflies are pretty incredible when you think about it, as they are able to move their four wings individually, allowing them to fly forward and backward, up and down, and may hover in mid-air. The hummingbird is equally amazing, being the only bird capable of flying as the dragonfly, including hovering in one spot. Both of these, of course, simulate the movements of a helicopter.

So the line, "Put in below the home of Brown," means precisely what it says. Literally enter below the Charlie Brown Spring, and the only manner in legally doing so is to put in, or touch down, by helicopter. It was then I heard the poem's first line gently whispering to me, "As I have gone alone in there." Ahhh, perhaps he flew in alone after all.

The trip was not a complete fail, however. We found a radiantly gorgeous lake, savored by only a few scattered travelers. It was right out of a magazine. Do people still peruse magazines? It was straight off the computer, then, from one of those fancy sites that show radiantly gorgeous lakes being savored by only a few scattered travelers. A calm serenity overwhelmed us both, as we basked in God's creation.

We drove back to the hotel. I was bummed, but not giving up. In our fourth floor room, I grabbed my phone and researched the word *marvel*, from the line, "But tarry scant with marvel gaze." Wonder, astonishment, filled with surprise, great admiration, amazed curiosity, gaze...the usual. Then I ran across Andrew Marvell, the 17th Century poet and good friend of John Milton. He wrote a popular poem called "The Garden", which speaks of life in the Garden of Eden, or Paradise. Near the end, it mentions a sundial and the sun above.[11]

On another page, I noticed a photo of a Marvell (two l's) sundial, comprised of a metal sphere upon a stand. An arrow ran through the entire sphere with an arrowhead sticking out from one end and feathers from the latter. I found this rather interesting, for two reasons. First, the most prized possession of Forrest Fenn, if I recall correctly, is an arrowhead he found when he was a little boy. This single arrowhead launched his passion and life pursuit for artifacts, particularly Indian antiquities. Secondly, I believed the blaze was a rock replicating an arrowhead.

I apprised my wife and showed her the picture of the Marvell sundial. "I'm going to the lobby for a drink...be back in a bit."

I strolled down the hall to the elevators and pressed the down button. As I waited, I turned around and saw something that floored me, if you will. A marvell sundial was sitting on a table across from the elevator! I had not noticed it before, but it practically yelled at me now. As the elevator

lowered me past each floor, I saw a unique object of decor on a table at each level. Our floor just happened to have a marvell sundial, complete with metal sphere, stand, and arrow.

Coincidence?

NEW REVELATION

O ur time ran out and we had to return home. A few additional points were gleaned during the next couple of weeks. Forrest attested that people are going to be surprised when they realize where the chest is hidden. That seemed a valid statement, realizing its challenging spot to reach.

I pondered the passage, "But tarry scant with marvel gaze." Without examining deeper, it seems to be telling the searcher to tarry (linger) scant (little), with marvel (astonished) gaze, or *linger little with an astonished gaze*. But we now know a marvell was a type of sundial. The sun's rays would shine upon the arrow portion of the sundial, and cast a shadow below. Now if the blaze assumes the shape of an arrow, as I believe, then it seems the sun should shine upon the rock blaze, and inevitably cast a shadow below its point.

The "linger little" did not make much sense to me, so after a little study, I discovered that tarry also means to *remain* or to *stay*. Now this gets interesting. Scant generally means little, meager, slight, restrict, or diminish. Nothing exciting there. So I kept digging. Scant has another meaning, one rarely suggested. A scant is a masonry term depicting a large rock which is cut vertically on both sides. The Y sliced into the mountainside rock seemed to fit. I needed to tarry scant, or *remain in the vertically cut rock* of the Y, if I am to find the chest.

Let's back up to line four of the poem, "And hint of

riches new and old." New riches were a given, as we seek a present, modern hidden treasure. Older riches were a bit trickier.

I investigated further. Roughly fifty miles south of the Y were the ghostly murmurings of riches from an older time. A remote area of the Bighorn Mountains in Johnson County is named Hole-in-the-Wall. Notorious gangs hid along its narrow passes in the late 1800's, including Butch Cassidy, the Sundance Kid, Jesse James, and the Logan brothers, amongst others. The geography was perfect for a lifestyle of thievery, for it was secluded and virtually impossible for lawmen to get near without the bandits knowing.

Millions of dollars, in today's value, in both currency and gold, was brought here from bank robberies and train heists. "Hint of riches new and old." I was sold. Now ninety percent certain I had unearthed the proper spot, I was ready to return to Wyoming. I just needed one thing... a helicopter.

SECOND TRIP

M y second trip to Wyoming was a solo trip, one month after the first. I flew into the quaint town of Cody, and was met by a cowboy security guard at the airport. Decked in boots, massive belt buckle, and cowboy hat, he was straight from an old western. What a welcome. I loved it!

I grabbed my bags and hopped into my airport rental car. After getting a few last-minute supplies in Cody, I drove east to the quaint town of Greybull, and then turned south toward Worland.

Upon being abandoned the following afternoon, I watched the helicopter fly away. It morphed into a fly, and then a dot, before vanishing. I felt mildly terrified. Alone, far from human life, and no cell service, I began setting up my tent, if you can call it that. It resembled more of a coffin, slightly longer than I am tall, and two feet high at max. It was tapered both inward and downward toward my feet, and gave me an eerie feeling that this may be the end. My first time ever assembling a tent, I began to panic as the sun descended faster than ever before.

I knew a bear or mountain lion would come running out any moment, and I was ready, with bear spray
and a small 38 calibre—just enough force to make an angry
bear, super angry. With the onslaught of night, I climbed
into the tent and lied down. Trust me, it was no easy task
clambering in. I had to enter slowly, feet first, and shimmy
the rest of my body carefully, without compromising the
structure of the tent. I was being shoved into a nylon can-
non like a human cannonball.

What if I sleepwalk during the night and step off the
nearby cliff? I have never sleptwalked before, but there is a
first for everything. In fact, I had to look up the word *sleptwalked* to see if it is even a word, and sure enough...another
first for me. The horrid thoughts persisted.

As I lay there an hour, a breeze arose. Being an amateur camper, I made an epic fail in where I parked the
tent...if you can park a tent. I staked it in open grassland on
top of a ridge, close to a wooded area. I figured the grassy
field would be safer, with fewer animals lurking for lack
of trees and brush. The wind picked up hurriedly. Though
anchored to the ground, my tent soon became a kite, toss-
ing from side to side in the bitter wind on top of the
world. Flapping furiously, the raucous between wind and

tent would not allow me to sleep. An hour passed. Then another. I continued looking at my watch, knowing I needed sleep. A third hour sailed by.

Leaves crackled a few feet from the tent. It was a slow and methodical crinkling of dry leaves. What is out there? Do I unzip my flimsy coffin and peak out with a flashlight? Or is better to remain within and hope it prowls past? Intentional steps continued beyond the tent. Why wouldn't it leave? "Go away!" I yelled. Would it run away or pounce on my tent and dash me to pieces? I heard it again. "Go away!" I hollered in the deepest, manliest voice I could muster.

I had to pee. Middle of the night. I waited. Pitch black outside. What would I encounter outside? I cannot go out there. I felt like a child, afraid of the dark, and rather than turning on a light, the lad pulls the cover over his head. Flipping on my flashlight, I searched for an empty water bottle. I can tinkle in the bottle. Found one! Wait, I have never done this before. I crinkled the bottle a little as I surveyed the small opening. What if I miss? This tent is way too claustrophobic already to risk a urinary blunder. I held on.

I could hold it no longer! Creeping out into the night with a flashlight and bear spray, the most amazing cascade of pee ensued. What a lovely spectacle the universe observed that evening. I can only hope a satellite image captured the breathtaking moment.

I glanced at my watch. Four hours have been lost and the wind was not abating. My eyes were heavy. Five hours. I heard another animal outside, but this time it was definitely a slither, and I could hear it slowly lurking alongside the tent. It would stop, then continue, stop, and continue. I was freaking out, and tried shouting at it, to no avail. I slapped frantically at the side and bottom of the tent. There was no way I was going outside! For some reason, I felt safer inside, as if a snake was unable to bite through cheap nylon. It finally left or stopped moving, one or the other, I could not be certain. Six hours slinked by. Seven. I eventually drifted, after lying in a ravaged tent for seven and a half hours during a mild tempest.

Daylight was approaching, and I was thankful for the three hours of sleep. It was time to get up and begin the hike. Once outside the tent, I heard a slight rustling, a calculated movement around the other side. It was the exact sound I heard during the night. Peaking over, I saw what it was...leaves! You have got to be kidding. Unfamiliar-looking to me, each lonely plant stood only inches from the ground, and boasted about five huge dry leaves apiece. With a breeze, the dry leaves grazed one another like giant tortilla chips scraping against each other. I swear it sounded like a mountain lion casually sneaking past. I was yelling at dry leaves last night.

Wow, the scenery was impressive—endless skies, peaceful prairies, and dense, green forests. I decided not to take Forrest Fenn's route exactly. I'm no moron. You see, I found a shortcut weeks prior on an internet map.

Grabbing my backpack, hiking poles, metal detector, and pistol, I began the narrow descent down the mountain ridge. I carried plenty of food, water, a flashlight, extra batteries, clothes, bullets, a knife, inadequate first-aid, and my phone, for I had taken computer screen shots of the area weeks prior.

The beginning of the hike was pleasant, as the downward slope showed mercy on me. I trailed a charming dry creek bed, dotted with river rocks, jutting out repeatedly amidst grass and weeds. I speculated how cheerful and lively it must look as water manipulated its way downstream certain times of the year. Hundreds of years of erosion has a way of carving a stunning tapestry upon a terrestrial canvas of sod and soil. Too much? I digress.

As my progress continued, my excitement grew. I was finally approaching my target, the justification for these two trips and time invested in the chase. Rocks grew larger and weeds matured into twisted, tangled brush. Slopes dipped more abruptly and unpredictably, causing me to veer off path haphazardly. My friendly trek grew burdensome and more strenuous the further I descended. As I climbed down a large boulder, a hiking pole slipped and I toppled flat on my butt, my heavy backpack plucking me to the ground like a magnet. It seemed like something was working against me the closer I drew, impeding my journey.

I happened upon a large animal skeleton resting on the smooth rocks of the dry creek, weeds weaving through its ribcage, neck, and skull. At least it's an animal, not human. But then I considered, how am I supposed to make it, if this large animal could not survive its natural habitat? I bid it adieu. Rest in peace, dear friend.

Almost there. I can see a lone, slender evergreen tree, flourishing proudly amidst two steep embankments of rocky cliff on either side. The chasm was so confined, the tree likely brushed the rock face on each opposing side. I believed the purpose of my mission lay at the base of that tree or slightly beyond it. I stopped suddenly, 30 paces from the tree. A small drop-off emerged at my feet, and another one 20 paces ahead of that one, just before the tree. A brushy terrace rested between the two steep declines.

If I jumped down the first descent, I may sprain an ankle or break a leg. But even if I landed fine, I could not tell how far the second dip dropped. It could prove more dangerous than the first. And if that is true, I may not be capable of climbing back up the steep incline from which I jumped. I could be stranded without cell service, or worse, die of an injury before anyone ever found me.

I *am* a moron, I concluded. I should never have attempted a shortcut! But the aerial view map made the hike appear so effortless. What a deceiver, an internet map can be. I surveyed my surroundings. I recalled Forrest Fenn's reassuring words, that if he was standing by the chest, he would see mountains, trees, and animals, and smell pine needles and pinyon nuts, or something like that. I observed mountains, animals, and pine needles. I have no idea what a pinyon nut is, but I suspected I was the only nut out here.

I rested on a spacious boulder near the foot of the drop-off, contemplating my next move. Do I go for it, and risk my life? Or do I attempt to hike back up? I was not even sure I could scale a couple of the inclines if I did choose to return. It is much easier to go down than up, I reasoned. I thought about my wife and children. How I wished I was home, instead of stranded between two perils. Quit being a big baby! I sat and prayed for a while, and at last, decided it was not worth the risk to continue downward. The chest was no longer an issue at the moment. I would be elated to simply make it back to my tent coffin.

On the ascension uphill, I observed the animal skeleton again, finding relief in seeing my friend once more. After a challenging hike and a few rests, I reached the tent. Setting my backpack down, a snake scurried from beneath my tent and ventured away. It was small, but I know younger venomous snakes are often more dangerous than adults. Mature snakes have the courtesy of releasing your leg once they have injected venom in you, but the young ones hold on and empty their venom entirely, like a toddler in his terrible two's, recklessly releasing his fury upon mankind.

Oh, heck no! I may or may not have said heck, that part is murky. It may easily have been the h-e-double hockey stick word in the heat of the moment. I ran after the snake and mauled it with a hiking pole. I am not having a repeat of last night!

I crawled into the tent to lie down, and it tore. Used for both hiking and killing, I now braced the hiking poles in the tent for structural support. Oh, the many uses a tool assumes when the need arises.

I did not imagine it possible, but that evening was worse than the first. The temperature dropped considerably, much more than the prior night. Prepared I was not, for a cold summer night. I failed to anticipate the need for a sleeping bag, nor did I possess a sleeping mat. My hips were aching from constant rubbing between hip bone and buried rocks beneath the tent. I knew right then and there, camping was not my thing. Hotels are infinitely more comfortable.

I squirmed into five shirts, three short-sleeved and two long, slipped on three pairs of socks and a pair of work gloves. My solitary blanket was puny, more like a blankie. A newborn baby would have loved it. Confronted with the decision of covering my feet or neck, but not both, for that was no option, I chose my neck, with feet exposed. I was freezing!

A frigid rain began falling, and my teeth chattered uncontrollably. I imagined basking in the afternoon sun, and that tricked my mind for only a few seconds. The chattering continued, and I wondered what it took for hypothermia to set in. I exhaled my warm breath beneath the mini blanket. I read later you are not supposed to do that, as it will accumulate moisture and actually make you colder. My ears became enraged for neglecting them in the cold.

I reached for my bag, and my face skimmed the top of the sinking tent. I had no idea a tent could perspire in the rain. It came deprived of a rain fly, to deflect rain from the actual tent, so ice cold rain was sweating through a dreadfully drooping tent, ever increasingly assuming the likeness of an actual coffin. I was unable to roll over without brushing freezing rain upon me.

Unzipping my bag, I grabbed a pair of clean boxers, and pulled them over my head and ears. And there I lay, unable to sleep once more, teeth trembling, three pairs of socks, thermal underwear and pants, five shirts, a baby blanket with feet exposed, work gloves, and underwear on my head.

Times like these compel a person to ponder life. I reflected many years back on the morning of one of my birthdays, July 11, 2000, only months after committing my life to Christ. I awoke and sauntered to the bathroom. On the counter, sat one of those daily flip calendars, presenting a Bible verse to consider for that particular day. I clearly remember flicking the light on, and praying, "Thank you, God, for giving me life."

I immediately flipped the calendar upon finishing my one sentence prayer and read the verse for that day. "But life is worth nothing to me unless I use it for finishing the work assigned me by the Lord Jesus—the work of telling others the Good News about the wonderful grace of God" (Acts 20:24).[12] It kind of freaked me out and I'll never forget it. I doubt it would have been as meaningful had it not begun with the word, "But," as I heard God's immediate response to my prayer. It humbles and moves me to evaluate what significance my life is or isn't having beyond this present world.

By the grace of God, I did not wake up dead. I emerged from my tent after a short nap, and wandered to the edge of a bluff. Scanning the horizon, I assessed my predicament. Reaching the chest location would necessitate hiking around a lengthy mountain ridge, descending upon the far end, and following the weaving river in the deep canyon below. I would then need to spend time actually searching the area, and retrace my steps all the way back.

There was clearly insufficient time before the helicopter would return for me.

I turned around, and to my surprise, a vulture was flying unusually low, right toward me. It flew directly overhead, and circled around to glide above me once again. It was so close, we caught each other's eyes, the most beautiful bedroom eyes I ever saw.

No, not true. My wife's eyes are actually the most beautiful I have ever seen. These were far more vile and repugnant. Immediately, a second vulture silently drifted over my head. A third, moments later, descended and soared just above me, and circled back for another gaze. Did I look that dreadful? I waved my arms and shouted at them. I am confident a person's sanity hangs by a single loose thread numerous times during a lifetime.

While awaiting the chopper, I discovered a rock in the shape of an arrowhead, maybe six inches long, closely resembling the blaze. Snapping a photo, I wondered if I would ever make it beneath the blaze, "look quickly down", and cease this darn quest.

Returning to the small Worland airport required flying over an extensive area of dry and desolate hills, devoid of vegetation or any other signs of life for miles and miles. It was a dusty-brown desert region, where one might suppose he was on mars had he known no better. It was a bittersweet flight as we retreated from my purposed destination. But things could have been worse.

The pilot recounted an incident a few months prior, while he was soaring over the same landscape. He noticed a tiny red dot in a sea of sandy tan dirt, far off in the distance below, and descended to investigate. Drawing near, he realized it was a red pickup truck, turned over on its side. The driver had apparently missed a turn on the dirt road that skirted the cliff, and plummeted to the base of the rocky hill. Hovering above the truck, he noticed the driver's door open, but nobody inside or around. He called in the license plate number and discovered the driver and truck had been missing for months. The authorities combed the area, but found nothing. Sadly, he would not have made it out of the vicinity alive without help.

Thankfully, we made it back safely, and I could only hope to return once more and cross the vast wasteland to reach my site. I had no choice but to return. It was calling me back. "Aaron," it whispered beyond the rotating blades of the chopper. "A-A-ron..." Okay, I was tired and needed sleep.

The first trip drove me five miles shy of the chest. This trek led me within a scant 120 feet. I find it frustratingly comical that I journeyed 1300 miles to reach this precise location, a distance of 6,864,000 feet from my home, only to be hindered the final 120 feet. A few feet can make all the difference. I'm getting closer, I assured myself...third time's a charm.

PHANTOM

I could not believe I returned to Texas empty-handed. I knew precisely where I needed the chopper to drop me off next time. Next time? A third trip? I sought God once more in prayer.

"God, if you want me to go back, and charter a helicopter again, I'll do it, but I need more certainty the chest is hidden where it is. I can't imagine what else can be gleaned from this poem, but I don't want to look like a fool!"

In reality, if God wants us to complete a task, we are to do it, with or without the proof we desire. That is faith, and we should trust his direction regardless of personal reason or logic. Even so, I wanted further confirmation before telling my wife I was headed back. I did not want her thinking I had established a second family up there.

God quickly showed me something from the lines:

"If you are brave and in the wood
I give you title to the gold."

This line reminds me of the ever popular line from Winnie-the-Pooh, by A.A. Milne. Christopher Robin tells Winnie-the-Pooh, "You're braver than you believe, and stronger than you seem, and smarter than you think."[13] The Winnie-the-Pooh series began in the 1920's, when Forrest Fenn was just a young lad. So this, like Charlie Brown, is assuredly nostalgic to Forrest.

The adventures of Winnie-the-Pooh take place

within the Hundred Acre Wood, also known as The Wood. This area of woods was inspired by the Five Hundred Acre Wood of Ashdown Forest in England. The Five Hundred Acre Wood was sold off from the rest of the Forest in 1678, and it remains privately owned today. Consequently, this area is not very accessible to the public, much like the parcel of land in Wyoming surrounded by private property. A sketch of the Hundred Acre Wood map even depicts a small river snaking its way through.[14]

In the final chapter of the Winnie-the-Pooh stories, from the book, *The House at Pooh Corner*, Christopher Robin is leaving, and all of his friends know things are not going to be the same anymore. Some readers believe Christopher is going away to school for an extended time. Others think he is becoming an adult, and will be losing interest in his childhood bear. It also seems to hint that he is older now and possibly going to die soon, much like Forrest believed he was from his bout of cancer years prior. All of Christopher's friends gather around, and Eeyore proceeds to give a speech, a surprise poem, called *Poem*. It is a farewell poem for Christopher. It's interesting that Forrest penned a poem similarly for all to ponder.

Christopher takes Pooh to a special place, an enchanted place, amidst the Forest and a cluster of pine trees. From here, they could view the entire world around them. Christopher hopes Pooh will visit him in the enchanted place from time to time, and wants Pooh to promise to never forget him.[15] This sounds remarkably similar to Fenn's enchanted spot in the woods, a special personal place, and the location he originally intended to die. Forrest clearly desires for people to visit his enchanted place, at least at some level, and for his legacy to live on through his poem and promise of hidden treasure. The portrayal of the enchanted place and approaching death of Christopher Robin, both occurred in the final chapter, or chapter ten. However, this chapter is actually titled in Roman numerals, or Chapter X. Not compelling by any means, but amusing since hidden treasure on a map is often denoted with an "X".

What I saw next was fascinating. Forrest has stated that only the phantom knows where the treasure is hidden. Now I knew the front cover of Fenn's book, "Too far to Walk", depicted the shadow of a man gripping a staff. This must represent the phantom, I concluded. But that is as far as I took it, nothing more...until one day, I zoomed in on the area map. I decided to pivot the map 180 degrees, to gain a unique perspective on the layout and geography of the land.

That's all it took. I gleaned new clarity, like never before. I told my wife I am now ninety-nine percent certain the chest is hidden in our location. I could never be one hundred percent sure without visibly seeing it, so I allowed a one percent potential for error, to guard against excessive disappointment in the case I was mistaken. Not to be confused with pessimism, it was my attempt at remaining a realist.

I showed her the inverted map. The shadowing of

the Y, when reversed, replicated the shadow on Fenn's book cover. I was beside myself. I found the phantom! Both legs, torso, head, and hat in the photo mimicked the shadows created by the cliffs. The curvature of the figure's left arm was reflected in the dark shade, too. Why, there was even a staff! You can tell the satellite image was taken mid morning, as shadows were cast toward the west. The photo on the book was likewise captured with the sun at a similar degree of height in the sky, though difficult to determine if it was snapped in the morning or afternoon.

There was one difference between the photo on Fenn's book cover and the shadowing of the cliffs, however. The landscape shadow did not clutch the staff as it did in the book's photo. Instead, the walking stick bolted straight up from the shadow's left shoulder. I figured it couldn't be perfect, but was represented closely enough. The odds of finding a figure, with a hat, and a stick at all, amongst all the other clues seemed too coincidental to be inaccurate.

I then stumbled upon something Forrest once said in regards to a particular artifact in his collection. The piece was a twelve inch tall wooden figure of Thoth, an ancient Egyptian deity, that dated back to around 6th century BC. Boasting the body of a man, and the head and beak of a bird, it held a bronze scepter in its left hand. Forrest said it is not supposed to be holding a scepter, but indeed it was. He pointed out that sometimes it is the aberration of an artifact that lures the collector.[16]

I looked up the word *aberration* for clarity in this context, and I was all the more intrigued. An aberration can be a state of abnormality, like a delusion or an oddity. It may also imply something different from what was expected, perhaps a deviation, departure, or distortion from how something ought to be.[17] A *scepter* is basically a fancy staff carried by a ruler, representing power. Bingo! The cliff's shadow outlined a staff, or scepter, stemming from the figure's shoulder, a deviation from the book's photo, where the figure is holding the staff in his hand.

Another short poem by Forrest Fenn, found in *The Thrill of the Chase*, is entitled an "Ode to Peggy Jean" (Forrest's wife), and speaks of three creatures flying overhead. I believe it is referring to either his body or the hidden chest, or possibly both, depending upon when he penned the poem, since he originally planned to die alongside the treasure. It speaks of a sparrow with secrets fluttering by, an intentionally focused raven flying overhead, and finally his shadow soaring past. The shadow, in particular, seemed odd to Fenn in his poem, as he pondered why it did so.[18]

This conveys to me, of course, the birds witnessing the location from an aerial perspective. His shadow wanders past, or above Fenn's enchanted place, each and every day the sun travels from east to west. The phantom shadow calmly drifts over the chest, beneath the blaze, as the sun strolls beyond the towering cliffs above.

Forrest insists no one will find the treasure by accident. The one who discovers it will travel to the location in confidence. I finally possessed this confidence.

WAITING

I promptly sought to return to Wyoming, and yet another roadblock emerged. Few helicopter services exist in the area I needed to reach. One refused to help me to my destination. Supplying crop dusting and pesticide services by chopper to neighboring private landowners, they did not want to jeopardize upsetting their clientele in the chance I was actually going to hunt on the public property. Again, the private landowners possessed a monopoly on the public land, since it was landlocked by surrounding private land. I assured them I would not hunt, nor do I possess a desire to hunt. No sale. They would not take the risk.

The company I originally chartered was fully booked. August through October were hectic months, as they were desperately needed to help extinguish fires throughout Wyoming and Montana and other states. Forests were dry and uncontrollable fires were plentiful. The need for helicopters showering buckets of water was understandably more urgent than my wish to go camping again in the middle of nowhere.

Meanwhile, the evenings in Wyoming grew colder as the days drew shorter. I would need to wait eight months until summer to attempt another trip. God was teaching me virtues a person is unable to learn from books or the experience of another. Some things one must learn on his own. Humility, patience, and trust were but a few. And if there is one thing I have learned over the years, you never want to pray for patience or other virtues, unless you welcome challenging moments and times of testing. God rarely awards an individual proper character without the person doing his part, as God seeks to refine and sanctify the soul.

Speaking of prayer, how can a person effectively pray and be heard? I'm still learning as the next, but a few elementary elements emerge to me.

First, what is the holiest of prayer positions? Thankfully, there's not one. Jesus prayed standing. Jesus prayed sitting. Jesus prayed while hanging on the cross. One may rightfully pray while kneeling, driving a car, skateboarding, or swimming under water. The position is not essential, as long as the appropriate attitude and reverence exists. One must be completely surrendered to God, wanting his will above one's own. When this occurs, our prayers are unselfish and better aligned as the Spirit moves us to pray more appropriately.

There's a story of a man who asks his preacher if it was fitting for him to eat while he prays. The preacher responds, "Oh, no! Never eat while you pray! Have respect for God while you commune with him." A few days later, another person asks the same minister if it was suitable if he prays while he ate. The minister eagerly replies, "Of course, we should pray without ceasing. It's always a great time to pray!"

What about the classic folding of hands in a holy posture of prayer? That does nothing to arouse God, I assure you. I love how Jesus often looked up to heaven when he prayed. His attention was riveted upon his Father in heaven, looking upward with eyes open. I rarely close my eyes when praying anymore, for the simple reason I remain more focused and alert, and less likely to get sleepy.

If God influences you to pray persistently about

something, by all means, do so. But Jesus specifically warns against praying repetitiously. God is not enticed by the number of times we redundantly pray. God hears and is enlivened by a repentant spirit and desire to obey him.

Effective prayer can move God. It is not that we change God's mind or his feeling toward a subject or request, but rather a change is inspired in *us*. It then becomes fitting and appropriate for God to answer the petition as it aligns with his will. This is key.

Anyway, back to the quest. My wife, Andrea, lovingly decided to travel with me. I say lovingly, for she in no way desired to go, but she did not want me to die out there alone. Suddenly, I felt relieved about a potential mountain lion attack. I now simply needed to outrun my wife in case of an intrusion. Obviously I jest, and I speculate she would likely surpass me in flight. But I find comfort in numbers, and the odds are improved in warding off a potential attack with the presence of two people.

We needed to prepare for the upcoming trip. We purchased a roomier tent that was simple to set up, and sleeping bags that zipped up like mummies, for a cozier night sleep in the cold. Waterproof and snake proof boots would help in case we needed to cross a shallow creek or tread through thick brush. Wool socks, mini lanterns, and a water filter were also added for comfort and convenience, and a satellite phone for emergency.

Andrea confessed to me her confidence level in our location for the chest...a paltry ten percent! I was appalled! But I figured, at least it was in the double digits. And on the bright side, if we do discover the treasure, she will be all the more surprised.

This trip would prove a little different than the last. Since I was hindered from venturing further down the mountain the prior year, we determined to approach the site from an alternate path. We would begin at the base of the canyon and hike up next time. But we needed to wait until the following summer to return to Wyoming. So we waited. And waited. And waited.

Until the day I decided to test my own faith. Spurred with inspiration, I penned this book months prior to our third trip to Wyoming, before ever unearthing the treasure. So while most of this book is complete, the ending remains a mystery, as of this writing. Perhaps I write in vain.

And when I concluded all I was able to pen prior to our third trek into the mountains, I set my computer aside, and waited some more.

THIRD TRIP

T he sun was hardly ascending as we descended into the 1000-foot chasm, monstrous cliffs enveloping on all sides. We were a speck, in light of towering mammoths of endless rock and forest. The pilot spiraled the helicopter slowly downward toward the base of the canyon. Wholly surrounded by private land, this was the only way the public could legally enter the public property. An enlivened grassy clearing welcomed us below, just large enough to safely land. My wife and I grabbed our backpacks as we departed the chopper, and the mini meadow danced excitedly beneath the whirling rotor blades.

The enormous dragonfly calmly lifted as we waved farewell. The pilot gestured back with a smile. We would see him soon enough, as we were merely exploring for the better part of two days and one night. Scanning the area, I felt insignificant amidst the dramatic landscape. Nature has a way of rousing both awe and humility.

We slid on gloves, hoisted our backpacks, and set out with trekking poles to reach our destination of just over one mile. Studying the area from our home computer, we simply needed to trail a small river *up creek* that wove along the canyon bottom. No human trails were anywhere in the vicinity, but this should prove easy enough.

A charming little creek immediately emerged, trickling into the river we planned to follow. Looking back, I'm embarrassed at how long it took us to cross, as one could easily jump across *without* a backpack. Wearing snake boots with shafts extending just below the knees, we feared overflowing them with icy cold water. When searching for boots prior to the trip, we discovered a choice must be made, to either select a tall water-proof boot offering little protection from snakes, or else snake-protected boots lacking water-proof quality. Fearing a snake bite with no medical attention available, we opted for a somewhat water-proof boot with great snake protection.

So finally crossing the miniature creek, we made our way through tangled thickets and reached the North Fork Powder River. We headed upstream for a couple of dozen yards before being forced to cross to the other side. A steep wall of rock to our right grazed the water's edge and climbed three football fields in height. We waded in with hiking poles, careful to avoid slipping upon the slippery polished river rocks below. Fish, I assume trout, swam feverishly away from us in the clear shallow stream. A tree had fallen towards the center and extended to the far side. We clambered on top and gradually sauntered across, each step carefully calculated, as the weight of backpacks and slick tree trunk worked against us. Time and water boast a manner of molding a perilous slime along drenched wood. I hurled my backpack a few feet ahead of me onto the bank to aid my sense of balance. Once I crossed, my wife tossed her pack towards me. Then, stepping out onto the log, I reached my hand to offer support. We made it!

Wandering further, it was not long before we knew we must cross back once more. The bank grew suddenly steep, and we had no choice but wade through the chilly river. The hike proved grueling. Trees hovered overhead bearing gnarled roots weaving across and downward into the brook. Boulders loomed, jutting out wildly to sip from the cool waters, demanding we splash and stumble to the other side again and again. Centuries of erosion had littered the canyon with massive chunks of cliff chipping apart from the heights above.

I grew discouraged and stopped, turning to Andrea. "I had no idea we'd have to cross this many times," I confessed. I scanned the rough terrain all around. "Drea, how in the world could a 79-year-old hike to this location and back, twice, in one afternoon?"

"I don't see how either," agreed my wife. "No way."

I studied the river ahead of us. "I know Forrest was in great shape, and he was used to hiking in rough areas. But even so, I can't see how he could have." My spirit sagged. I felt guilty for convincing my wife to join me out here, in the middle of nowhere, miles from any sense of humanity.

"We've come this far," my wife promptly replied with optimism. "We're going all the way, no matter what!" I needed to hear that. Knowing she was in good spirits reinforced my confidence and inspiration to press on.

After a while, we approached another cliff base that sauntered out into the river, again mandating us to plod across. Fish darted excitedly. The center of the river deepened more than we wished, in light of our knee-high boots, so we waded upstream a bit while hugging the craggy cliff. Years of erosion from the water's current sculpted a hollow indentation along the wall of rock, extending over the river. I am certain we appeared affectionate toward the smoothed rock face, as we embraced it while scurrying along the water's edge.

Back on land, we trudged a bit further, until the bank compelled us to ascend a small rise to skirt around an enormous boulder blocking our path. The rise was cluttered with a jumble of sticks and branches strewn about.

My hiking pole spooked a small snake, who hurriedly whisked away beneath a pile of twigs. I was told previously there were no snakes in such high elevation! We shimmied past, relying on our trekking poles more than ever, from warding off snakes to potentially dueling cougars.

We finally arrived at our targeted spot, after zig-zagging across the river a dozen times. A dozen times! The same thought kept wrestling our minds. How could Forrest have walked this far, returned all the way back, and then turn around and do it again? Did he really cross the river 48 times, in one afternoon, at age 79, while shouldering the burden of both chest and gold, at least a portion of the trip? It didn't seem plausible.

But we made it and my excitement surged. We began searching immediately, with metal detector in hand. Roaming away from the river, we ventured into the base of the Y between two intimidating cliffs. Our slight ascension proved brief, as a steep slope appeared, maybe 150 feet from the river, blocking us from exploring further uphill. Resembling a long, thin slide, the smoothly weathered rock surface veered vertically perhaps 100 feet. The sharp upward incline proved even more threatening with a steady trickle of water dribbling down its slippery slope. The tight, narrow passage was bound and hemmed by an abrupt cliff on each side, preventing a further climb uphill.

Gazing to the top of the rocky slide, we observed the top of a lone tree. The display was both familiar and disheartening. At the peak, stood the same tree I witnessed the prior year on my descent into the Y from the top. We were helpless in reaching it from the bottom up as I was unable from the top down. Could the chest be hidden in the tiny parcel so inaccessible near the tree?

We combed the modest area below for two hours, to no avail. My mood plunged. My despair heightened. Initially planning to camp at this location, we decided instead to trek back to the original drop-off site. It promised a more suitable terrain of flat grassland to set up tent and rest for the night. But first, I had to scour the area once more, just in case I overlooked something. I searched again, metal detector leading the way, moving logs and rocks and brush.

Nothing. I had to accept it. Abandoning the site in order to return proved emotionally painful. I was admitting defeat and giving up. I struggled to fight off emotions, as I felt strangely embarrassed in exposing my grief before my wife. And again, it was not for the sake of the money not found, but for lost opportunity. I still aspired for God to validate his promises through me, that others might believe. Why would God lead us all this way to encounter failure?

The walk of shame is all too real. To commit time and money and a dream to an endeavor with confidence, and discover disappointment instead, rouses a personal shame and humiliation. We hiked back down the 150 feet toward the river and stopped at the bank, staring at the water. It had only been three hours since we arrived at this spot, but things were strikingly different. The river was angry. Perhaps annoyed at our presence, furious with our probing, or offended at who knows what. It seems everyone and everything is so easily offended these days!

We assessed the span of water in our means to navigate across. The clarity of the water had vanished, and we could no longer see the river rocks lining the bottom. Fish were no longer visible, as the current had grown deeper and swifter. We had never anticipated a transformation in the river, especially one so suddenly.

After some time contemplating our options in crossing, we stepped into the river, slowly and methodically with hiking poles. We manipulated each slippery rock in the dark watery abyss below, mindful of leaning into the current to remain balanced. We sighed as we reached the other side, strolled a a few dozen yards, and reluctantly crossed back over again.

We ascended a rise to avert a giant boulder gracing the water's edge. Debris had fallen from the trees above, forming a thick layer of fine sediment upon the steep slope. The lack of any flourishing grass along the incline encouraged a likely landslide to any who ventured near. Not knowing the peril before us, my wife began the ascent up and around the boulder. The powdery silt proved too loose and she began an uncontrollable and gradual slide down toward the massive rock. It was little benefit to brace one's hands into the ground, for they, too, would begin to glide, as loose earth sunk lower. Her body paused in the miniature grainy avalanche.

"Don't move!" I hollered. "I'll go further up and back down the other side." The ground appeared more stable just beyond Andrea. The massive boulder was so close to the base of the slope, a dark crevice formed, awaiting the unfortunate victim. If she continued sliding, my wife could easily get wedged into the cleft, just wide enough to fall within, and narrow enough to be entrapped. I grasped at occasional tree roots and clung to low-drooping branches, gently sliding along the way. Finally managing a secure footing on the far side of my wife, I reached out as far as I could. Andrea crawled, as delicately as possible, awakening a flurry of fine sediment dribbling down toward the dark abyss below. We seized one another's hand

and held on tight. She wormed her way over, as I pulled her to denser ground, safely from the mouth of the rift.

It was time to navigate across the river again. We scanned up and down the limited span of water for a calm ingress. After much contemplation, we agreed the current was much too swift and dangerous to attempt. I imagined my wife slipping on the slick river rock and being swept downstream, and then helplessly slamming her head against a boulder. It wasn't worth the risk.

We decided to remain there for the night. The weather was gorgeous today, with plenty of blue skies and sunshine. This year was a bit abnormal in the northwest, as more snow lingered in the mountains at this time than usual. We determined the sunny day generated a great deal of snow melt further up north, thus causing the surplus of water. A substantial reservoir of water resided only a few miles upstream, with an outlet pipe flooding excess water downstream as necessary. So this made sense why the river swiftly transformed, and we reasoned, would settle back to normal during the evening in the absence of sunlight. We would be able to continue our return hike the following morning.

Even while hemmed in between cliff and raging river, we discovered a perfect little shelf to pitch our tent about 30 feet uphill. Surrounded by trees, the quaint spot offered shade and a soft bed of organic debris to sleep upon. It was a tight spot, though, and a massive boulder leaned over us on one side. If it fell, we would likely be crushed and never found. But it seemed sturdy enough. The height of our intimate campsite also lent safety in case the river below were to flood.

We set up a two-person tent on our tiny stranded parcel of land. Once inside, we unraveled the sleeping bags and got as comfortable as possible. After a light snack, Andrea pulled out two photos, neither of which I knew she had brought. She began sobbing, and glancing over, I saw photos of our two daughters. Oh, what did I do in bringing my wife with me to this dangerous spot? Urgent prayers emanated throughout the night for God's hand of protection, provision, and peace.

That proved a difficult night, wrestling between fear and trusting God. The river below drowned all other sounds. Every time I awoke, which was often, the crashing of the enraged current struck anxiety within me. What if the water did not recede in the morning? How would we return for the helicopter pick-up? What if no one finds us, and we end up perishing? What would happen to our children?

We awoke to the vulgar rushing of whitewater beneath us. No! Surely the water had retreated during the night. We unzipped the tent and crawled out, hopeful of what transpired below. Stepping to the ridge beyond the tent, we glanced down at the river. The level had not receded at all! The torrent mocked us as it surged passed in a frenzy. Why had it not gone down? Andrea found the photos of our daughters again and tears gushed. My eyes watered as I struggled to suppress my concern.

After eating a few bites, for lack of appetite, we surveyed along the river bank for a possible entrance. The flow was too threatening. We would never make it back to the helicopter pick-up spot unless the current abated. A minor panic seemed intrinsic at this point, but thankfully we had rented a satellite phone for such a scenario.

Unfortunately, reception was all but nonexistent at the base of the canyon, between two thousand-foot cliffs on either side, trees everywhere, and monstrous clouds

continually drifting overhead. With fewer branches hanging over the river, I carefully stepped onto the furthest
rock jutting out from the bank in hopes of gaining a better
signal.

Satellite phones boast the ability for reception
from the many satellites orbiting around the globe. But
we had such a miniature thread of visible blue sky at any
given moment, the probability of accessing a satellite was
miniscule. Reaching both arms out over the rapids, I tried
and tried to gain reception. I dared not lose my grip of the
phone as I clung tightly. A phone call was out of the question, I soon realized. It would have to be a text to the pilot.

Obtaining a green signal every once in a long while,
I hurriedly typed a message, or attempted to send a saved
message. Reception was lost in only a few seconds, so getting out any manner of message was nearly impossible.
Nearly. After several hours, and exhausted arms, I was
finally able to send parts of texts, that together I hoped
would make sense.

I explained our dilemma to the pilot. The Dull Knife
Dam was a few miles upstream, governing the amount of
water released through the canyon. If they could pause the
outflow, or at least minimize it for a couple of hours, we
could then safely return. The pilot confirmed that was not
an option, so finally, I swallowed my pride and affirmed
we needed a rescue. That proved a humbling resolution for
me. The last thing I wanted was to admit I was not man
enough to get my wife and I back to safety, and besides, the
thought of ending up on the main news thread of the internet made me squeamish. I envisioned us being air-lifted,
but the trees and cliffs were so high, it seemed unrealistic.

Certain another stranded night was in our future,
we left our tent pitched. I was pleasantly curious later

when I believed I heard the faint sound of chopper blades in the distance. Could it be? It was! The chopper drifted high above the river and passed over us. I grabbed a bright yellow jacket and red shirt, and climbed onto a modest boulder for the next fly-by. Seeing it approaching, I waved the colorful items to catch the pilot's attention. It flew on and did not return. How did he not see me?

Minutes later, I heard Andrea holler from our campsite thirty feet above me. You had to yell to be heard over the rumble of the rapids. "Did you say something?" she asked.

"No!" I hollered back.

A minute later she shouted, "Did you call me?"

"No!" I shouted again. I stared up at her in confusion. Has she gone mad?

Suddenly, a figure dropped down near my wife from a small overhead crag! It was a young man decked in comfortable hiking attire, backpack, and a thick primitive staff for balance. How did he find us so quickly? How did he find us at all? A second climber plopped down from the rock face above, similarly dressed, with a broad welcoming smile. What a beautiful sight they were!

My wife and I hurriedly disassembled the tent and threw random items into our packs. We brimmed with a euphoric shock, realizing we were getting out of here immediately. A safe and comfortable hotel room would be awaiting our arrival later this very evening. It was as if we were stranded for months. It had only been the better part of two days, but we are not outdoor survivalist kind of people. It was not our fault, for we were bred for comfort, for safety, for warm beds.

The two guides led us back to our original drop spot, across the winding river, up and down slopes, and through a carnage of trees and thickets. They were explorers, and in their element, reveling in a remote wilderness while rescuing a couple of castaways. Upon revealing we were from Texas, the lead guide explained that he had just been to Texas the week prior. He attended someone's graduation about an hour away from our residence in College Station. What were the odds?

Throughout the hike, two more rescuers remained 1000 feet up at the top of the bluff, while two others waited with the pilot at the pickup destination. All carried professional two-way radios, and kept in continual contact with one another. Upon reaching the chopper, we were all flown to the top of the mountain ridge where the others awaited. Three pickup trucks, a six-member volunteer rescue crew from the Johnson County Search and Rescue squad out of Buffalo, a helicopter pilot from the Worland Municipal Airport, the county sheriff, my wife and I, and a search and rescue dog all stood in a circle in a stunning green prairie in the middle of nowhere.

Everyone was cheerful and chatting with one another. Unbeknownst to us, a torrential rainfall had showered much further up north, causing the river downstream to surge. As the sheriff scribbled information from us, I removed my snake boots and turned them upside-down. A flood of water gushed from each boot. "Did you get that fish?" asked the sheriff.

I was exhausted, so it took me a few seconds to realize he was joking about the volume of water I had accumulated from the river. We all laughed. They were all in such good spirits. You could tell they cherished the outdoors and loved doing what they do, helping people in need. The camaraderie amongst the group of men was genuine and charming. It was reminiscent of a nostalgic beer commercial, replete with pick-up trucks, an enthusiastic dog, and a band of cowboys alone on the range, recounting adventures and reveling in the good times. The only things missing were a campfire, some cold ones, and a catchy jingle compelling you to head for the mountains.

We said our goodbyes and waved farewell as the chopper ascended and our fellow compadres dwindled into dots upon the grassland. A cocktail of emotions welled up within me. A deep feeling of dejection emanated as once more we drifted away from the location I felt certain sheltered the chest. Embarrassment in needing to be rescued, and disappointment in another failed pursuit weighed heavily. But mingled with these emotions, was a joy and relief in being safe and alive. An odd cocktail of solemn thankfulness befell.

CONFIRMATION

S oon after returning home, I stumbled across a website I had not before seen. It cited a collection of scrapbooks from Forrest Fenn himself, each chronicling a personal story or tale from his lifetime. Many searchers presume each memoir simply paints a portrait of the life of Forrest Fenn. Others are convinced the greater than two hundred and fifty journals whisper hints of the treasure chest's resting place.

A danger lurks in matching hints with a person's specific solve of Forrest's poem, so confirmation bias naturally runs rampant. Coincidental clues are fabricated and bent to suit the assumptions of the seeker. I recognized this potential allure, but there were just too many coincidences to dismiss.

Since Forrest's journals will naturally make more sense to those familiar with his writings, and less to those unacquainted with them, I will simply mention the particular scrapbook (SB) number and associated hint without going into considerable detail. The following grabbed my attention the most, and *of course, these are all my opinion.*

SB   9: Photo of Forrest with bunny ears behind his head (two fingers forming a Y).[19]

SB   27: 2 parrots facing northeast (location of Bighorn Mountains in Wyoming).[20]

SB 46: Cowboys lost to Broncos by three points (Northeast of the chest location is a large aerial number 3, formed by a small creek and an array of trees.).[21]

SB 49: Emphasis on CLOVES (The LO in this word contains an upside-down 07, possibly hinting at both the 07 and the upside-down shadow, or more probably, I'm reading into it too much!).[22]

SB 54: Bronze jar with dragonfly and butterfly on it (both may hover or fly in any direction like a helicopter).[23]

SB 56: Clouds kissing ground (Cloud Peak in Bighorn Mountain range). three 300' long ships (number 3 again).[24]

SB 82: p 3-30 written on comic cover (3's). Comic book covers relay that comics were meaningful to Forrest (Charlie Brown, Winnie-the-Pooh).[25]

SB 83: 3 wives, 300 friends (3's). "a smile in his heart" (treasure near the heart of the shadow). Sitting Bull (Sitting Bull Park is nearby).[26]

SB 86: "itching powder in Skippy's shorts"; photo of itching powder (North Fork Powder River).[27]

SB 90: Broken arrowhead in the eye of a buffalo skull (blaze resembles arrowhead). Cody references (Wyoming).[28]

SB 92: Mummy cave by Cody, Wyoming.[29]

SB 98: "move a few things from my closet to the basement" (downward movement). Photo of Forrest sitting on loose rocks (loose rocks in and around chest area).[30]

SB 99: 3 mirrors in Fenn's bathroom (3).[31]

SB 100: Stick figure running with football toward the right (stick figure is upside-down Y with football serving as the treasure, hinting the location on the right as one enters the Y from the north, progressing downward. The left leg is lifted similar to the shadow's figure).[32]

SB 107: More hints in this scrapbook than any other, imo, due to it being SB 107, containing 07, hinting at being "tired and weak". The jumbled phone line and "I forgot to plug my idiot phone in" both hint of bad reception, which is definitely accurate in this locale. Chaotic silverware placement is organized to face both the north and east, signaling the northeast of Wyoming, while all forks are facing north, hinting at the North Fork Powder River. The pen and pen cap are, likewise, facing northeast, similar to the 25º angle on a compass. "always a write way to do something" (misspelling the word "right" lends suspicion to it really meaning "wright", as in the Wright Brothers, further suggesting a wright way to do something, or the necessity of one to fly to the location). The upside-down $5 bill speaks of the upside-down figure's shadow, while the bill precisely creased to allow one to still read "public and private" on the note, hints at the challenge of legally journeying beyond both public and private property to reach the chest. "Mr. U Puceet" on the envelope translates "Up You See It", suggesting the blaze (arrowhead cliff rock) directly above the treasure. The 1921 address is referring to the year 1921, while the stamp with fireworks refers to July 4th...together, July 4th, 1921. The final scene of one of my favorite movies, *The Shining*, zooms in on an old photograph of Jack Nicholson at the July 4th, 1921 ball at The Overlook Hotel. An overlook is key. "to my 'location'" definitely refers to the secret hiding spot. "robbed a bank" (One meaning of bank is a steep slope. Fenn's spot is certainly on a slope.). "A cab brought me home" refers to C.A.B. (Civil Aeronautics Board) who probably revoked Forrest's pilots license due to his age. "I don't ever plan to drive again." (Forrest does not plan to fly anymore.).[33]

SB 109: Red clovis knife from the Bighorn Mountains.[34]

SB 111: Huge 3 on magazine cover (3).[35]

SB 113: 2 1/4" lure (1/4, or quarter, or 25, hinting at the 25º portion of a compass, out of the 360º), pointing northeast, or the Bighorn Mountain area. "lure doesn't look like much, but please don't let his appearance mislead you." (chest location may not be as beautiful as other places, but it's still more significant to Forrest). "Claude Ivey" (helicopter pilot).[36]

SB 115: Photo of toothbrushes. Neither photos of Forrest and Brad Pitt smiling show any teeth (treasure in teeth of the Rockies, or a rocky mountainous ridge resembling teeth). "when I'm home alone" (In the movie, Home Alone, the boy takes a toothbrush from a store without paying.). "Sonja Jane Pulver" (Sonja means wisdom; Pulver is a German word for powder, hinting at the North Fork Powder River).[37]

SB 116: "fox in bottom right" (Forrest advises looking for things that stand out in the area solve via an aerial perspective of Google Earth.).[38]

SB 117: "many miles from a road on a friend's ranch in northeastern" (secret spot is several miles from the nearest road within the ranches of others in the northeastern region of Wyoming). "A mile or so farther, as we walked along a softly flowing stream of water" (walking down into the Y, one follows a miniscule, dry creek, that becomes a softly flowing stream of water when it rains). "70 pounds" (07 backwards...tired and weak).[39]

SB 122: Retired from Air Force in 1970 (07 backwards). "arise about 0430 and go teach students how to fly airplanes (43º latitude...north and south coordinate as a plane climbs up and down). "morning of the 7th" (07).[40]

SB 124: "a few fault lines in my aptitudes" (The Y sort of consists of two fault lines becoming one, stemming north to south, or latitudinally...latitude instead of aptitude.). "with it he took my photo. I mean he took my photo with it" (he flipped the wording around). 28" rainbow trout (rainbow = 43º latitude. A rainbow ring always centers in the sky opposite the sun, about 43 degrees in radius. The sun may not be greater than 43 degrees above the horizon. 28" hints at 58 'in both latitude and longitude when flipped upside-down). "11 lbs" (lbs, or #, refers to the number 3 on a keyboard. So 11 times 3 = 33, or 33" latitude). "6 lb tippet" (tippet, or tip it, is possibly hinting at flipping the 28" again).[41]

SB 125: "3rd Street" (3).[42]

SB 127 / 127.1: The Jungle Cock bird is mentioned many times (JC for Johnson County, WY). All sorts of fishing flies portrayed. One fishing fly actually appears to be suspended above Forrest's poem in one photo (helicopter needed).[43]

SB 129: Forrest received a $1000 bill *thirty-three* years ago, with a 1933 date on it (I believe they produced these bills in 1928 and 1934, but not 1933...3's).[44]

SB 130: Title: "Not Tired Yet" (Tired = 0 and Yet = Y). "on our last leg" (of shadow). "Our place is near his recliner in the den. Got that?" (a den can be a hollow or cave used as a hideout). walking shadow...Hope you're taking notes (hints given). 3 toes showing in photo (3).[45]

SB 132: Photo of envelope has a July 4th stamp (like SB 107). The date stamped on envelope is 07 FEB 2015 (07).[46]

SB 138: Photo with FW-582 on side of jet, and 53582 on tail (58', or 58 minutes, for both latitude and longitude).[47]

SB 140: "3 foot deep pond" (3).[48]

SB 146: "hummingbird...dart back and forth, and hover" (only bird with similar movements of a helicopter) "Tail End Charlie" (Charlie Brown Spring). 3 ducks, 3 inches tall, $3 each (3's).[49]

SB 147: The two feathers in John Moyers' painting resemble the southeastern portion of the Bighorn Mountains and region of the chest site.[50]

SB 148: Photo of Forrest with *both legs* in front of fireplace (depicting top of Y).[51]

SB 152: "narrow the gap" (gap of the Y).[52]

SB 163.5: FW-582 on side of jet in photo (and 53582 on tail) once more.[53]

SB 166: "path that led down" (take path down into the Y, as opposed to up). "into the pot, I put the lid on, placed it reverently into the ground, and covered it up with dirt. Then she started piling rocks on the grave. She kept piling them on." (chest is possibly placed just beneath the ground surface and covered with rocks).[54]

SB 169: "3 winners", "3 blocks" (3's).[55]

SB 170: "do something right" (wright brothers...need for helicopter). Paintings of clouds (Cloud Peak). I ordered chicken fried steak with the gravy on the side, and no veggies (The chest is the gravy on the side of the locale that lacks vegetation...the secret spot is indeed an area of rocks).[56]

SB 171: Bell tower at excavation site (Bell is a helicopter manufacturer).[57]

SB 172: Bell tower behind home (Bell helicopter manufacturer again).[58]

SB 173: 28" portrait (SB 124 speaks of a Rainbow trout of 28" in length, or 58 when flipped upside-down).[59]

SB 174: Photo of an old, dull knife (Dull Knife Reservoir a few miles from site).[60]

SB 175: 70 pound rooster (07).[61]

SB 177: "Lady Peace" is written on airplane sketch (peace and Y). Painting of clouds (Cloud Peak). Drawing on napkin is turned around, as the artist's signature is backwards, hinting to look at things from a different perspective (upside-down figure's shadow).[62]

SB 180: "It was a subterfuge" (The stick figure is a trick, or disguise, to hide something. In this case, the figure represents the upside-down Y.) "teetering to the starboard side" (chest on the right-hand side).[63]

SB 181: "Battle of the Little Big Horn" (Bighorn Mountains).[64]

SB 182: A northeast chinook (Bighorn Mountains located in the northeast Rockies). A chinook is a warm, dry wind.

It is also a helicopter, as in *Boeing Chinook*). "northeast of Pecos and up. Up to 10,637 feet." (The Bighorn Mountains are in the northeastern portion of Wyoming. 106º denotes degrees longitude).[65]

SB 185: "3 pounds" (3).[66]

SB 188: "I thought it must be an aberration." "ladder that climbed straight up about 10 feet". The "staff" portion of the shadow is an aberration, that does not exist in Forrest's shadow on his book cover. The ladder is similar in being long and narrow. Dizzy Dean and Satchel Paige are famous baseball pitchers. The Bottom Note in the scrapbook mentions he uses commas wrong. One meaning of comma is a small difference of *pitch*. Other meanings of pitch are slope and incline (chest is located on a slight slope).[67]

SB 190: J.C. Penny (JC for Johnson County).[68]

SB 191: Photo of upside-down airplane (upside-down shadow). "They cleared us to enter a right base leg...advised us to enter a right base leg for the north/south runway." (Hike down the right leg of the shadow from the top of the ridge. The shadow runs north to south when upside-down.).[69]

SB 198: "survivor at the base of a 1000' karst cliff on the North East side" (Bighorn Mountains are in the northeast of Wyoming. This particular locale boasts 1000' cliffs, and the location of the chest is on a slope.).[70]

SB 199: "3-hour event". The winner was a 22 year old, though Forrest said it was a 23 year old. (3 stands out twice).[71]

SB 201: "I was closing down for the evening" (direction to

take into the Y).[72]

SB 202: Forrest mentions Yellowstone (Y), and in the same paragraph, he writes, "...right out of *Treasure Island*, You can't make this stuff up" (uses a capital Y for You in the middle of the sentence).[73]

SB 203: Book published in 2007 (07). St. John's College (JC for Johnson County). "three years" (3). Forrest adds a sentence at the end of first paragraph, that in my opinion, did not need to be there: "Yeah, it's just like Eli to do something like that." (Begins unexpected sentence with Y.) Then, in the final line of this scrapbook, Forrest again adds an oddly unnecessary sentence: "Your turn Eli." (Another Y).[74]

SB 204: Forrest once more adds a peculiar and needless sentence: "Yes, I still remember." Beginning with a Y, it correlates with this scrapbook's title, "West Yellowstone, as I remember..." (with another Y in Yellowstone). "north of town...usually had to drive off the road...for a few minutes" (north and off road both true).[75]

SB 205: 1/4 psi: Many scrapbooks reference 1/4, 1/4th, and a quarter (coin). I believe the quarter hints at the 25º portion of a compass (out of 360º), pointing north/northeast, or the Bighorn Mountain area. 3" white goat (3).[76]

SB 208: Gold locket on Suzanne Somers' golden necklace rests in the center of her chest (treasure hidden near chest area of shadow).[77]

SB 209: Another uncanny sentence: "Why is that?" (Y is that). "demoted angels" (go down). "beneath the understated colors" (down). A photo depicts a doll lifting its foot off a chest, and holding a small book entitled, "Path to

Perfect Happiness" near its torso (The treasure is near the torso of shadow. Perhaps someone stepped right over the chest, or very close, without realizing it.)[78]

SB 210: Joseph Cestmir (JC for Johnson County).[79]

SB 211: "about 58,688 times before" (hints at 58'...both 58 minutes latitude and longitude). "awkward looking box elder tree" (box elder trees grow fruit having seeds sometimes known as *helicopter seeds*, since they possess winged seed elements). "thank that great box elder tree for giving me inspiration." (Forrest loved flying helicopters, and I believe (don't quote me) he stated he would like to be a helicopter pilot for a living if he were to relive his life.) Bobby McGee (BM for Bighorn Mountains).[80]

SB 212: "glass partition...pheasant-under-glass...celebrated glass paperweight collection...served glasses of chilled" (other glass meanings include: to enclose, to wall, and to reflect). 3-piece suit (3).[81]

SB 213: 3 leaves in leaf collection (3).[82]

SB 214: "May 23, 1985" (Possibly hinting at seconds latitude...5-23-1985 = .5231985 x 60 = 31.39191 seconds). Sketch of figure with a note under his arm reads, "TOP SECRET". Only "TOP SECT" is bolded in black, however (treasure is located in the "top section" of the shadow, not the legs). "doodle tipped in" (tipped hinting at flipping the shadow upside-down). "A friend in Cody" (a nod to Wyoming). John Connally (JC for Johnson County).[83]

SB 215: "3 rules" (3). In group photo, legs of people are on the bottom of picture, while Forrest is located in the upper center (treasure located in central region of shadow).[84]

SB 216: *John* Whitaker Photography; *John Something* (Johnson County). The last etching shown depicts an Indian with *two feathers* in his hair (resembling a Y). Detailing possible reasoning for Forrest only keeping this one etching from his original set, Forrest concludes, "Maybe that's why I've kept this particular etching." (that's Y).[85]

SB 217: Signs that read, "DO NOT GET OFF THE ROAD. I didn't." (stay along the shadow's path). "143,000 soldiers were killed" (more were actually killed than that, so I feel it hints at the 43º latitude coordinate).[86]

SB 219: "drove about 15 blocks down hill" (hike down Y, not up). 3 pastors (3) 3 ladies (3). John (Johnson County). "riding it down the road" (hike down Y). 8" above asphalt... V-8 engine (possibly hinting 8" longitude coordinate). 19,139 miles (19139 is the Philadelphia zip code, where Sylvestor Stalone was victorious in the iconic movie, *Rocky* (treasure is hidden in a *rocky* area...okay, probably a stretch, but interesting nonetheless).[87]

SB 220: Drawing of two female stick figures. One is wearing a green dress and pointing both hands down (hike down the Y; green dress hints at treasure hidden in torso of shadow, not the legs or head areas). The other woman is wearing a red dress, while pointing both up and down. 1/4th page ad (25º on a compass once more).[88]

SB 221: "in broad daylight" (not in canyon near river and trees, but higher up the slope in a clearing). One sketch portrays a female stick figure wearing a green dress (treasure in torso area of shadow), and holding a fishing pole up (resembling the staff of the shadow) with a fish dangling in the air on a hook (the fish is the treasure).[89]

SB 222: One sketch depicts a female stick figure with a red dress (shadow does not have a dress), one male stick figure with a red head and not wearing a cap on his head (not near shadow's head), and two male figures wearing caps with green torsos (green for good or go to the torso area of shadow, which is wearing a shadow hat). Another sketch shows a female stick figure with a green dress who caught a fish (the fish being the treasure in the shadow's torso). Another sketch depicts a dog with an exaggeratedly long body, between its front and back legs. The obvious hint is the long torso, where the treasure is hidden within the shadow. Still another sketch shows a woman wearing a green dress, swinging a golf club in the air, with her left leg raised in the air (This is a close representation of the shadow, with its long staff protruding upward. Her green dress hints the treasure is not hidden within the legs or head of the shadow, but the torso). Birdie on the 4th hole (4th).[90]

SB 223: Photo of Forrest in between two other men. Forrest says, "That's...me in the middle again." (The word "again" seems oddly out of place and unnecessary.) Five sentences later, he says, "That's where it is." (Another peculiar and needless sentence, in my opinion. Both sentences begin with "That's", and it seems to hint that the treasure is in the middle of the figure's shadow...that's where it is.) References to clouds (Cloud Peak). Charlie Russell Riders (Charlie Brown Spring).[91]

SB 224: Titled "Three Sevens and a Vacuum Cleaner" (lucky number 7, as in 07). "I was dealt 3 sevens" (3 and 07, or simply lucky number 7). 4th floor (hint at 25º on a compass). Charlie Davis (Charlie Brown Spring).[92]

SB 225: Titled "Young at Heart" (Y in Young; treasure near shadow's heart).[93]

SB 226: "3' to the floor" (3). "I had to go down stairs" (hike down the shadow).[94]

SB 227: "Every 4th day" (4th, or 25º on compass). "big slab of beef liver" (treasure near shadow's liver). "I heard a dull GULP" (treasure near shadow's throat/stomach).[95]

SB 228: In the painting of Alexandra, she is pointing to her chest area (treasure near shadow's chest). "a Purple Heart" (treasure near heart).[96]

SB 229: "thin wallet's shadow" (shadow of figure). Johnny Carson (JC for Johnson County).[97]

SB 230: "I instructed him to flip it" (flip the shadow...heads and tails). buffalo (Buffalo city in Wyoming). "on the 4th hole with a 7 iron...quarter" (4th and quarter for 25º on compass and 7 for 07).[98]

SB 231: Entitled, "Yazzi Yarnell Dolls" (double Y emphasis). one doll is 43" tall (43º latitude since it measures the height of doll, or 'north and south'). Second doll is wearing a purse with two swords criss-crossed on it, I believe, resembling an X. The same doll is holding an arrow, which is pointing directly below a buffalo on the first doll. So, the secret spot, or X, is below the town of Buffalo a bit.[99]

SB 232: "I said 'gulp'...Gulp" (treasure hidden near shadow's throat/stomach).[100]

SB 233: "3 days" (3). Flagstone jar lid was laying on the floor. "buried to its rim under the floor" with corn (the chest is filled with gold (corn), and is possibly covered with a thin slab of rock at ground level). emerald cross found with a metal detector (a metal detector will aid in finding the chest beneath the rocks).[101]

SB 234: Book on Lyndon Johnson (Johnson County).[102]

SB 235: "gave the appearance of walking downhill all the time" (hike down the Y). Bobby McGee (BM for Bighorn Mountains).[103]

SB 236: "7 spacious rooms" (07). "quarter-page item" (25º on compass).[104]

SB 238: "Rainbow Hand" (43º latitude).[105]

SB 240: Photo of Buffalo skull (Near town of Buffalo, Wyoming, and it resembles a Y). 7 men, 7 dancers (07). The final sentence speaks of peace (Y) on this planet.[106]

SB 241: 7 1/4th...8.25 miles (both 1/4 and .25 hinting at 25º on compass). "center coin is upside-down" (shadow is upside-down).[107]

SB 242: "nose is too high" (not near head of shadow). "she was right in the *middle* of what was culturally vogue" (One definition of *vogue* is "the leading place in popularity" (treasure is in middle of shadow). "up between his eyes" (One definition of *eye* is "something central: center"). "Inlaid in the right side" (One definition of *inlaid* is "set into a surface in a decorative design"...treasure is possibly set into the ground or beneath rocks).[108]

SB 243: Forrest's *treasured* dog, The Bip, is being held next to Forrest's chest. Bip "moved off of his pad and into my heart, and even closer if there was such a place...The Bip, as if the crown jewels had been injected into the name." (The Bip is the treasure chest, near the chest of the shadow).

3'...3 miles...3 hours...3 miles (again)...7 drawings (3 and 07). "His liver failed" (treasure hidden near shadow's liver). "placed a sandstone slab on top" (treasure possibly hidden beneath a rock slab).[109]

SB 244: Forrest's artist friend, Eric Sloane, painted a picture called "Gaspard Memories", but on the back of the painting, it is named "GASPARD MEMORY" (It should have been a Y. Gaspard means "treasurer").[110]

SB 245: "exactly 8 1/4 inches" (1/4, or quarter, hints at 25º on compass, or 8.25" longitude). "palette is 33 1/2 inches wide...measured it with my ruler also. Yup, 33 1/2 inches wide. I always like to be exact." (Yup contains both Y and "up". He says exactly and exact, emphasizing his precision in the number given. The 33 1/2 hints at 33.5", or 33.5 seconds latitude, with seconds denoting the precise location of the treasure.) Painting of clouds (Cloud Peak).[111]

SB 247: "Jolly Green Giant helicopter" (helicopter is vital). December 7, 1941 (07).[112]

SB 248: "7 decades" (07). "tantamount to climbing the Washington Monument with loose rocks on each step" (the treasure is in an area similar to the Washington Monument, on a slope and full of loose rocks below).[113]

SB 249: "Down town...hunkered down...gutting down" (Travel down the Y. A gutter can be a low area that moves surface water away, which is the very reason for the Y's formation over many centuries.) A buffalo skull commands one's attention in the top center of the photo with a light shining upon it (Y). The word "yard" is used three times. One meaning of *yard* has to do with driving into a confined or controlled area. This area is definitely restricted by being completely surrounded by private property.[114]

SB 252: Photo of moon with a cloud covering a mountain peak (Cloud Peak).[115]

Another hint, and for the life of me I can neither imagine nor find it, but I recall Forrest discussing scissortail and meadowlark birds. Perhaps he hunted them at some point in his life. It dawned on me that a scissortail bird boasts a body with split tail resembling a Y. After researching meadowlarks, I noticed they sport a yellow chest with a black chevron across the front. Together, the design and color scheme uniquely replicates the shirt of the cartoon character, Charlie Brown. Fascinating! Forrest is a creative man.

TWENTY TWENTY

I t was the year 2020. I remembered that Forrest at one time seemed a bit enamored with frogs. He fashioned several metal jars and bells with figures of frogs on them, and even included two golden frogs in his treasure chest. More and more, things were making sense. From an aerial view on a map, about one mile west of the Y within the mountain ridge, emerged a mammoth frog, formed by trees and mountainous ridges.

And quite ironically, the final clue I deciphered was regarding the puzzling Omega symbol many have speculated about for years. Forrest would leave this symbol every once in a while as an end mark at the end of a book or other writing. Omega generally means the ending, last, or finale. I finally noticed from the aerial map, that the *bottom*

portion of the mountain ridge, resembling a frog toward the west of the hiding spot, closely mimics an omega symbol! Why had I not seen these things before?

Then an event occurred which I believe was intended by God, and if not, certainly peculiar. One day, in mid-February of 2020, my wife, Andrea, counted two money bags from our cafe, representing two consecutive days of sales. Aside from other denominations, the initial bag contained $91 in one dollar bills. The second money bag, to her surprise, also included $91 in one dollar bills. Immediately following, she went to the grocery store and her bill total came to $91.91. She relayed all this to me later that day.

In an unrelated conversation that same afternoon, Andrea admitted that she was still not sold on returning to Wyoming with me the following summer. I explained that camping the next time would actually be fun, with no river to worry about. Our final trip would be the same I had taken alone, beginning at the top of the ridge and hiking downward. I now realized that I had actually walked passed the correct spot. There was no need to continue down to the lone tree after all, for the chest remained above it in the shadow's torso. The evening we spent last year was intimidating, I agreed, but this time would be different. It would actually be enjoyable.

Hours later, while lying in bed for the night, I recalled my wife's story of the four 91's earlier that day. I suggested we read Psalm 91, just for kicks.

The brief chapter began, "Whoever dwells in the shelter of the Most High will rest in the shadow of the Almighty." The word *shadow* promptly stuck out to me, since we would need to enter the shadow of a man's figure within the mountainside. I later looked up this same reference in my New King James Bible, and noticed it used the phrase, *the secret place*, instead of *shelter*. This was definitely Forrest Fenn's secret place we were seeking.

I then observed that I had circled the "Psalm 91" heading in my Bible, probably fifteen years prior. Thumbing through the pages, it remained the only chapter heading, or anything for that matter, in my Bible I had ever circled. At the very least, I found this interesting.

The following verses depict God as my *refuge* and *protector*, in whom I trust. "You will not fear the terror of night, nor the arrow that flies by day," it continued. Several nights over the previous two years on location were a bit terrifying, and the blaze in the poem I still believed to be the arrow-looking rock jutting from the top of the cliff far above the chest.

I read on. "No harm will overtake you, no disaster will come near your tent." What! It actually said *tent*!

"For he will command his angels concerning you to guard you in all your ways...so that you will not strike your foot against a stone." Arriving at our location necessitated us hiking down a long, rocky path, worn from years of erosion by a tiny creek sustained only certain times of the year.

"You will tread on the lion and the cobra; you will trample the great lion and the serpent." Two things we feared on our last trip included mountain lions and snakes. "Because he loves me," says the Lord, "I will rescue him; I will protect him, for he acknowledges my name..."

And if that were not enough, with the onslaught of the coronavirus at the time, God's words were more dearer. "Surely he will save you...from the deadly pestilence...You will not fear...the pestilence that stalks in the darkness, nor the plague that destroys at midday. A thousand may fall at your side, ten thousand at your right hand, but it will not come near you."[116]

Psalm 91 spoke volumes to me. I am convinced God continues to speak through his Word today, if only an individual will listen. While not wanting to journey alone into the Rockies, and everyone warning against it, I slowly determined I could do it if it came to that. God would be with me.

The closer the time came for returning to Wyoming, the more I felt comfortable with going alone. But on the morning of June 2nd, 2020, I sat at my desk feeling anxious about my upcoming trip the following week. I said a quick prayer, confessing my nervousness to God. I asked him to give me peace that comes only from him, with both courage and confidence.

Four minutes later, I glanced at my computer and it read 8:30am (central time). I rarely trade stocks anymore, but I still enjoy seeing how the dow opens up. With the market bell ringing at 8:30, I clicked refresh on my stock page. As the screen promptly refreshed, I thought I noticed that it closed up 91.91 points the day prior. What? I immediately googled the market close on June 1st, 2020, and sure enough, the dow had risen 91.91 points. Had it risen 91.92, it would have meant nothing to me. It could have been 91 and one hundred different decimal numbers. It might have been 92 and another one hundred options in decimals. And with the fluctuation in the market at the time due to the coronavirus pandemic and an unpredictable economy, the deviation could have easily been several hundred points up or down, with one hundred decimal options for every point in either direction. The odds of it being up precisely 91.91 were astounding. To most, a chance happening, but to me, God had answered my thirty second prayer in under five minutes. The specific timing of a matter is often as inexplicable as the answer itself, apart from the influence of God. A new calmness filled my soul.

The pandemic struck in early 2020, wreaking havoc upon the globe. Unemployment skyrocketed while finances plummeted, and hundreds of thousands of people dying around the world. As uncertainty swarmed, fears spread as swiftly as the infection itself. With so much panic, suffering, and loss, it moved me to ponder humanity's need for a God to provide and protect. He is sovereign and in control at all times, and while he often causes adversity, he certainly allows challenging times in our lives for the purpose of drawing us to himself. He knows it generally takes pain and hardship to awaken us to the need we bear for him.

I noticed so many people frightened, lonely, and hopeless. Why were so few desperate enough to fall before God for help? We all share the same necessity for God, yet so many of us lack the perception of urgency to fill that need. I had one of those heartfelt moments and was inspired to write the next few lines, which somehow evolved into a poem, as I pondered the perplexing love of God for me.

PERSP3CTIVE

I spit on Jesus, the Man, the Christ.
Struck his face, enjoyed it, I was enticed.
He calmly obliged, as if to succeed,
He was no God, look at him bleed!
I swore at him and cursed his name,
A branch of thorns shoved in his veins.

He studied me with saddened stare,
Blood seeping in his eyes,
I beat him with a leather cord,
Sharp bits of bone chastise.
His back shred easily with forty tries,
Spiked his hand, humanity in his cries.

I murdered the One who lent me breath,
I am to blame,
I sent the Creator to his death,
I'll bear the shame.

I recall him looking down at me,
While laughing in my soul,
He said he paved the only way,
That one might avoid Sheol.

He forgave me, he softly spoke,
I know not the slightest why,
For me he came, was his reply,
For me he came to die.

I reflect upon that tree, that day,
Reminds me of a mystery,
Knowledgeable tree of evil and good,
He crushed the devil on similar wood.

He took my guilt, confirmed to me,
I am completely free.
Forever I will live with him,
And he shall live with me.

I told the news to a friend of mine,
That he could have the same,
He'll take away your emptiness,
The void that's been aflame.

Hopes lifted, his yearning began to swell,
To be cleansed, restored, in God to dwell!
Defeat, oppression, to be removed,
Confusion at last to be reproved.

Purpose obtained, new heart, new life,
Eyes no longer blurred,
Simply turn to him and one will change,
What splendid words he heard!

He pondered intently, the gain to behold,
He listened to reason, much grander than gold.
Wiping his tears, for now he could see,
He looked up to God, "But what's in it for me?"

GRAND ELUSION

The likely coordinates of the chest were 43º 58' 33.5" latitude and 106º 58' 8.25" longitude, in the very heart of the figure's shadow. If true, the 8.25" was hinted from the very beginning when Forrest claimed the chest was at least 8 1/4 miles north of Santa Fe, New Mexico, where he lived. The area boasts amazing seclusion, gorgeous scenery, excellent fishing, and a rich Indian history with limited exploration, since the public parcel is inaccessible by private land confinement.

From an aerial perspective of the shadow, as shown in a prior photo, one can detect a cloudy white portion near the figure's stomach and chest. This portion of the figure is white due to a flood of white rocks, somewhat reminiscent of the base of Mount Rushmore, which Forrest has mentioned now and then. The picture shows a portion of the rock area which I remain confident the chest was found.

My excitement heightened each day, and I was scheduled to fly out before sunrise on June 10th. On June 6th, however, Forrest Fenn stunned me when he affirmed to everyone that the chase had come to a close. I was heartbroken! After the chest lay dormant in the Rockies for ten years, it was troublesome for me to accept someone discovering it mere days before my arrival. Why had God not allowed me to finish this pursuit I felt he had guided me toward, especially when getting so close? I wrestled finding peace with this reality, not so much for the loss of money, but for missed opportunity. For some reason, God did not want me to find Forrest's hidden chest. Fenn's treasure had eluded me once again, and once and for all!

The prior two years taught me patience, as my will was forced to await God's timing. He was now teaching me other character virtues I needed to improve. Trust, contentment, and thankfulness, regardless of present circumstance, stared me in the face and begged me to protest. But God is sovereign and his will is perfect, good, and infinitely better than my best attempts or wants.

God could have moved me to trek out a week earlier, he could have confused the finder, he could have hindered the finder in discovering the chest. But he chose otherwise. We are faced with tests throughout our lifetime, and we will have a choice between two reactions. We can either trust God and give him praise, even when we fail to understand why events occur, or rather turn against God in bitterness, resentment, or anger.

And so I determined to release it all over to God, for him to do as he pleases. I recently had a personal epiphany, and I now find inspiration in seeking God's will so that he is pleased. The Bible speaks of the devil roaming throughout the earth as a lion, looking for someone to devour. Of course, he wants to devour the one who is faithful to God. Those who are unfaithful have no need of being deceived, as they are deceived already. He tested Job in order to influence him that he might grow angry and abandon God.

But all the while, the Bible portrays God as searching the entire earth, in order to show himself strong to the one who is faithful toward him. So my aha moment surfaced when I realized that Satan and God are seeking *precisely* the *same* person, one for the intention of misleading, and the other with purpose to bless! How effortless it must prove for each of them to notice the faithful few, so it inspires me to follow God without compromise or unthankfulness when things go contrary to my way. I admittedly have much room to grow. But failing to find the chest myself, I can remain confident that God's purposes for me continue to play out in his perfect way.

And though I am unable to prove this precise location of Forrest's hidden treasure, the overwhelming evidence affirms the location. Similar to a belief in God, once an individual witnesses the wealth of evidence surrounding him, it is difficult to dismiss his existence. From the micro cellular level to the macro scope of the universe, and everything in-between, faith in the presence of God becomes both real and attainable.

SOMETHING MORE

E ach of us is pursuing *something more* in life. It is intrinsic, a part of our nature to want more, to attain something outstanding, something remarkable. We aspire to achieve something great, to realize a rich fulfillment and satisfaction in life. And there is little wrong with that. In fact, we were intentionally designed that way.

Treasures exist everywhere, and assume innumerable forms. Some strive for fame and status. Others pursue a prestigious job, money, or influence. Still others seek joy, peace, love, health, beauty, pleasure, or freedom. While these are not corrupt in themselves, any of these aspirations may swiftly become an idol in one's life. Anything we elevate in precedence above God is accurately an idol. It may be something good and moral, but an idol nevertheless, when we place more significance upon it than we do God. A spouse, a child, or an ambition for joy or beauty, may each be considered an idol if revered in an unhealthy manner.

In the first of the Ten Commandments, God warns, "You shall have no other gods before Me" (Exodus 20:3). There remains an emptiness within each soul longing to be filled, that may only be *ful*filled by God. A deep loneliness and unrest looms apart from God, and a lack of peace and joy prevails.

My entire perspective changed when I finally learned an inspiring principle affirmed over and over throughout God's Word. I challenge you to read *THE OR-*

ACLE: Universal Law of Prosperity Defying All Others, where I reveal and examine the prophecy proclaiming prosperity to anyone who fears the Lord. Again, this does not mean you will receive all you desire. Instead, by turning to God and away from sin, one gains the *favor of God*. We must leave the results to God and give him thanks regardless of the outcome. His will is perfect and good, whether or not we recognize it at the time.

Many will consider me naive, and the cause and effect of my prayers mere coincidence. Some will mock. Some will always mock. That's expected. It remains part of the beauty of free will we each enjoy.

Even so, a wealth of promises await the one who faithfully fears the Lord. Most will scoff at the principle of the Oracle, "others will cheerfully agree with its principles, briefly observe them, and shortly fall away from lack of faith and commitment. The majority will be easily distracted by the cares of this world and the illusions it boasts. Unfortunately, the mirage of this life is all too real for many to dismiss..."

"But a few, a scant few, I dare say, will pursue God passionately. They will observe the Oracle faithfully. They will fear God and love him for whom he is and not for what they might gain. In these God shall take notice, and pouring upon them his boundless favor and goodness, he will award the treasures of life."[117]

Most people *want* the favor of God. Who would not? But most are unwilling to *sacrifice* the immorality necessary to gain his favor. So on the whole, these would rather continue their wrongdoing rather than acquire God's blessings. It proves too large a sacrifice to achieve, so they continue living contrary to the ways of God, and yet, wonder why they never seem to secure his favor.

Forrest Fenn originally wanted to die in a remote spot he held sacred, clutching a small box, filled with treasures accumulated during the course of his lifetime. In a sense, we each do this. I am guilty as any. Granted, few individuals plan their life closure as theatrically as Forrest, but each of us aspires to build a repertoire of things to which we hold valuable. God cautions," lay up for yourselves treasures in heaven, where neither moth nor rust destroys and where thieves do not break in and steal. For where your treasure is, there your heart will be also" (Matthew 6:20-21).

Fenn was strategizing his death, with only his bones to remain shortly thereafter, alongside valuables he was incapable of taking along. All prized possessions would remain, and he would depart penniless, as will we all. Can that be the greatest treasure in life, to accumulate wealth for someone else to come along and cling to for a time, until it inevitably passes to the next? There must be more!

Our greatest treasure *must* be God. Not a distant, inaccessible Man in the sky we tip our hat to, but an intimate, relational Creator who yearns to be a part of us, his Spirit protecting, providing, and permeating through us, that he might further his kingdom, employing us as agents privileged to affect and alter eternity within the souls of humanity.

When a man or woman is truly broken and surrendered to God, it is that moment God fills and begins to use him for extraordinary things. But God waits for *us* to act first. We must come to him empty and destitute, completely lacking in self-sufficiency and self-reliance. "The Lord is near to those who have a broken heart, and saves such as have a contrite spirit" (Psalm 34:18). This involves more than shallow remorse for past wrongs. Possessing a contrite spirit means bearing a humble and repentant attitude, where a person forsakes his sinful lifestyle, and begins living instead for God and according to his ways.

I find it fascinating, while one person spends fifty years gradually drawing nearer to God, another may achieve the same in five minutes. It has much to do with the heart, surrendering our will for God's (thy will be done), and being thankful for how his will plays out in our life. A genuine mental change *now* is all that is required. Repent, turn from sin, and trust in Jesus as Lord and Savior. God will mercifully forgive and begin to transform that individual.

But do not linger, supposing you will commit to God later in life. "I am not interested in that today. I will live for myself, according to the desires of my heart. *Tomorrow* I shall surrender to Jesus, once I have had my fill." This line of reasoning is like resolving never to wear a seatbelt in the car. "I will strap a seatbelt on right before an accident occurs."

Too late. One never knows what may transpire tomorrow. You must be prepared today. Choosing to delay repentance is choosing to remain in rebellion toward God. Many will sneer. The majority will ignore the warning. The majority will always dismiss the forewarning.

Wrestle with God, if you must, but gut it out with him *today*. Settle your eternal fate before this night has passed. God awaits with open arms. You have little to lose, and everything to gain. Jesus claims, "I am the way, the truth, and the life. No one comes to the Father except through Me" (John 14:6). Jesus warns to "enter by the narrow gate; for wide is the gate and broad is the way that leads to destruction, and there are many who go in by it." (Matthew 7:13).

I find myself re-surrendering to God now and again, all that I have and all that I am, as the flesh and world creep in. And I continue to pursue a deeper, more intimate walk with God, seeking further repentance and submission, that the Spirit may more fully indwell this wreck of a man.

Forrest Fenn has single-handedly awakened scores of people to wander into the depths of nature, to explore a world so often neglected. What an inspiration he has been! When he was a young boy, Forrest discovered an authentic arrowhead, the first of countless. A passion to explore was immediately born, and the remainder of his life would be conditioned by that single arrowhead.

Still a child at heart, his creative genius bridged a cryptic poem with a treasure, cleverly hidden in an enchanted place, a nostalgic space dear to his heart. He has succeeded in kindling a fire of inspiration and hope to a throng of people. I appreciate Forrest's generous spirit in extending this challenge, and simultaneously inflaming an admiration for the outdoors. I remain grateful for the opportunity Forrest awarded me and thousands of others.

The treasure will certainly pass the embrace of its finder, as it has numerous hands before. But recognize one thing that is certain, that our worth is found solely in God. Ironically, it is *we* who are the treasure of God, though why I am unable to fathom.

He longed for *me*. He longs for *you*. He was mangled and murdered for us both. What an absurd concept, Creator dying for his immoral creation! I don't understand it. I definitely don't deserve it. But I cling to him for so doing.

No other treasure will compare to the life and blessing God offers. God is my prize, and his presence will I ever pursue. I pray a blaze burns within you for the one who lent you breath, and that your soul will thirst for something great, for something more.

This world is deceptive. Happiness is always up ahead. Contentment drifts just around the corner and forever beyond our reach. Success dwells close by, yet continually in the distance.

Do not be deceived! An array of treasures will forever entice in this present life. But one will stand apart, alone, and above all others, offering fulfillment in life, and restored fellowship with our Maker. The greatest treasure in this world is much, much closer than you think.

ENDNOTES

1. Fenn, F. (2011, August 23). In the Beginning. *Thrill of the Chase Blog.* Retrieved from https://daln-eitzel.com/2011/08/23/in-the-beginning/ (Permission to cite poem given by Forrest Fenn.)

2. Peanuts. (n.d.). In *Wikipedia.* Retrieved March 23, 2019, from en.wikipedia.org/wiki/Peanuts.

3. Brown, A. (2016). *The Oracle: Universal Law of Prosperity.* Bloomington, IN: WestBow Press.

4. Draw (n.d.). *Merriam-Webster.com.* Retrieved May 22, 2019, from www.merriam-webster.com/dictionary/draw

5. Gully (n.d.). *Merriam-Webster.com.* Retrieved May 22, 2019, from www.merriam-webster.com/dictionary/gully

6. Ravine (n.d.). *Merriam-Webster.com.* Retrieved May 22, 2019, from www.merriam-webster.com/dictionary/ravine

7. Sedan (n.d.). *Merriam-Webster.com.* Retrieved May 25, 2019, from www.merriam-webster.com/dictionary/sedan

8. Car (n.d.). *Merriam-Webster.com.* Retrieved May 25, 2019, from www.merriam-webster.com/dictionary/car

9. Airship (n.d.). *Merriam-Webster.com.* Retrieved May 25,

2019, from www.merriam-webster.com/dictionary/airship

10. Hybrid Airship (n.d.). In *Wikipedia*. Retrieved May 25, 2019, from en.wikipedia.org/wiki/Hybrid_airship

11. The Garden. (n.d.). In *Wikipedia*. Retrieved March 21, 2019, from en.wikipedia.org/wiki/The_Garden_(poem)

12. *New Living Translation*. Bible Gateway. Web. Retrieved on 9 May 2019.

13. Pooh's Grand Adventure: The Search for Christopher Robin. (n.d.). In *Wikipedia*. Retrieved March 25, 2019, from en.wikipedia.org/wiki/Pooh%27s_Grand_Adventure:_The_Search_for_Christopher_Robin

14. Hundred Acre Wood. (n.d.). In *Wikipedia*. Retrieved March 26, 2019, from en.wikipedia.org/wiki/Hundred_Acre_Wood

15. Milne, A.A. (1985). *The World of Pooh: The Complete Winnie-the-Pooh and The House At Pooh Corner*. New York, NY: Dutton Children's Books.

16. Fenn, F (2014, July 15). Gold is the Skin of the Gods. *Thrill of the Chase Blog*. Retrieved from https://dalneitzel.com/2014/07/15/ibis/

17. Aberration (n.d.). *Thesaurus.com*. Retrieved April 3, 2019, from www.thesaurus.com/browse/aberration?s=t

18. Fenn, F. (2010). *The Thrill of the Chase*. Santa Fe, NM: One Horse Land & Cattle Ltd Co.

19. Neitzel, D. (2013, February 25). Scrapbook Nine. *Thrill of the Chase Blog*. Retrieved from https://dalneit-

zel.com/2013/02/23/scrapbook-nine/

20. Fenn, F. (2013, March 24). Scrapbook Twenty Seven. *Thrill of the Chase Blog*. Retrieved from https://dalneit-zel.com/2013/03/24/scrapbook-twenty-seven/

21. Fenn, F. (2013, October 14). Scrapbook Forty Six. *Thrill of the Chase Blog*. Retrieved from https://dalneit-zel.com/2013/10/14/scrapbook-forty-six/

22. Fenn, F. (2013, November 15). Scrapbook Forty Nine. *Thrill of the Chase Blog*. Retrieved from https://dalneit-zel.com/2013/11/15/scrapbook-forty-nine/

23. Fenn, F. (2014, January 1). Scrapbook Fifty Four. *Thrill of the Chase Blog*. Retrieved from https://dalneit-zel.com/2014/01/01/scrapbook-fifty-four/

24. Fenn, F. (2014, March 11). Scrapbook Fifty Six. *Thrill of the Chase Blog*. Retrieved from https://dalneit-zel.com/2014/03/11/scrapbook-fifty-six/

25. Fenn, F. (2014, July 8). Scrapbook Eighty Two. *Thrill of the Chase Blog*. Retrieved from https://dalneit-zel.com/2014/07/08/scrapbook-eighty-two/

26. Fenn, F. (2014, July 12). Scrapbook Eighty Three. *Thrill of the Chase Blog*. Retrieved from https://dalneit-zel.com/2014/07/12/scrapbook-eighty-three/

27. Fenn, F. (2014, July 22). Scrapbook Eighty Six. *Thrill of the Chase Blog*. Retrieved from https://dalneit-zel.com/2014/07/22/scrapbook-eighty-six/

28. Fenn, F. (2014, August 16). Scrapbook Ninety. *Thrill of the Chase Blog*. Retrieved from https://dalneit-zel.com/2014/08/16/scrapbook_ninety/

29. Fenn, F. (2014, August 24). Scrapbook Ninety Two. *Thrill of the Chase Blog.* Retrieved from https://dalneitzel.com/2014/08/24/mummy_cave/

30. Fenn, F. (2014, October 19). Scrapbook Ninety Eight. *Thrill of the Chase Blog.* Retrieved from https://dalneitzel.com/2014/10/19/scrapbook-ninety-eight/

31. Fenn, F. (2014, October 20). Scrapbook Ninety Nine. *Thrill of the Chase Blog.* Retrieved from https://dalneitzel.com/2014/10/20/scrapbook-ninety-nine/

32. Fenn, F. (2014, October 22). Scrapbook One Hundred. *Thrill of the Chase Blog.* Retrieved from https://dalneitzel.com/2014/10/22/scrapbook_one_hundred/

33. Fenn, F. (2014, November 12). Scrapbook One Hundred Seven. *Thrill of the Chase Blog.* Retrieved from https://dalneitzel.com/2014/11/12/scrapbook-one-hundred-seven/

34. Fenn, F. (2014, November 17). Scrapbook One Hundred Nine. *Thrill of the Chase Blog.* Retrieved from https://dalneitzel.com/2014/11/17/scrapbook-one-hundred-nine/

35. Fenn, F. (2014, November 28). Scrapbook One Hundred Eleven. *Thrill of the Chase Blog.* Retrieved from https://dalneitzel.com/2014/11/28/scrapbook-one-hundred-eleven/

36. Fenn, F. (2014, December 9). Scrapbook One Hundred Thirteen. *Thrill of the Chase Blog.* Retrieved from https://dalneitzel.com/2014/12/08/scrapbook-one-hundred-thirteen/

37. Fenn, F. (2014, December 14). Scrapbook One Hundred Fifteen. *Thrill of the Chase Blog.* Retrieved from https://dalneitzel.com/2014/12/14/scrapbook-one-

hundred-fifteen/

38. Fenn, F. (2014, December 15). Scrapbook One Hundred Sixteen. *Thrill of the Chase Blog*. Retrieved from https://dalneitzel.com/2014/12/15/scrapbook-one-hundred-sixteen/

39. Fenn, F. (2014, December 19). Scrapbook One Hundred Seventeen. *Thrill of the Chase Blog*. Retrieved from https://dalneitzel.com/2014/12/19/scrapbook-one-hundred-seventeen/

40. Fenn, F. (2014, December 29). Scrapbook One Hundred Twenty Two. *Thrill of the Chase Blog*. Retrieved from https://dalneitzel.com/2014/12/29/scrapbook-one-hundred-twenty-two/

41. Fenn, F. (2015, January 11). Scrapbook One Hundred Twenty Four. *Thrill of the Chase Blog*. Retrieved from https://dalneitzel.com/2015/01/11/scrapbook-one-hundred-twenty-four/

42. Fenn, F. (2015, January 17). Scrapbook One Hundred Twenty Five. *Thrill of the Chase Blog*. Retrieved from https://dalneitzel.com/2015/01/17/scrapbook-one-hundred-twenty-five/

43. Fenn, F. (2015, January 24). Scrapbook One Hundred Twenty Seven. *Thrill of the Chase Blog*. Retrieved from https://dalneitzel.com/2015/01/24/scrapbook-one-hundred-twenty-seven/

44. Fenn, F. (2015, January 30). Scrapbook One Hundred Twenty Nine. *Thrill of the Chase Blog*. Retrieved from https://dalneitzel.com/2015/01/30/scrapbook-one-hundred-twenty-nine/

45. Fenn, F. (2015, February 3). Scrapbook One Hundred Thirty. *Thrill of the Chase Blog.* Retrieved from https://dalneitzel.com/2015/02/03/scrapbook-one-hundred-thirty/

46. Fenn, F. (2015, February 22). Scrapbook One Hundred Thirty Two. *Thrill of the Chase Blog.* Retrieved from https://dalneitzel.com/2015/02/22/scrapbook-one-hundred-thirty-two/

47. Fenn, F. (2015, May 9). Scrapbook One Hundred Thirty Eight. *Thrill of the Chase Blog.* Retrieved from https://dalneitzel.com/2015/05/09/scrapbook-one-hundred-thirty-eight/

48. Fenn, F. (2015, May 16). Scrapbook One Hundred Forty. *Thrill of the Chase Blog.* Retrieved from https://dalneitzel.com/2015/05/16/scrapbook-one-hundred-forty/

49. Fenn, F. (2015, September 28). Scrapbook One Hundred Forty Six. *Thrill of the Chase Blog.* Retrieved from https://dalneitzel.com/2015/09/28/scrapbook-one-hundred-forty-six/

50. Fenn, F. (2015, November 1). Scrapbook One Hundred Forty Seven. *Thrill of the Chase Blog.* Retrieved from https://dalneitzel.com/2015/11/01/scrapbook-one-hundred-forty-seven/

51. Fenn, F. (2015, November 11). Scrapbook One Hundred Forty Eight. *Thrill of the Chase Blog.* Retrieved from https://dalneitzel.com/2015/11/11/scrapbook-one-hundred-forty-eight/

52. Fenn, F. (2016, March 18). Scrapbook One Hundred Fifty Two. *Thrill of the Chase Blog.* Retrieved from https://dalneitzel.com/2016/03/18/scrapbook-one-

hundred-fifty-two/

53. Fenn, F. (2016, November 2). Scrapbook One Hundred Sixty Three Point Five. *Thrill of the Chase Blog.* Retrieved from https://dalneitzel.com/2016/12/20/scrapbook-one-hundred-sixty-four/

54. Fenn, F. (2017, February 2). Scrapbook One Hundred Sixty Six. *Thrill of the Chase Blog.* Retrieved from https://dalneitzel.com/2017/02/02/scrapbook-one-hundred-sixty-six/

55. Fenn, F. (2017, March 12). Scrapbook One Hundred Sixty Nine. *Thrill of the Chase Blog.* Retrieved from https://dalneitzel.com/2017/03/12/scrapbook-one-hundred-sixty-nine/

56. Fenn, F. (2017, March 30). Scrapbook One Hundred Seventy. *Thrill of the Chase Blog.* Retrieved from https://dalneitzel.com/2017/03/30/scrapbook-one-hundred-seventy/

57. Fenn, F. (2017, April 4). Scrapbook One Hundred Seventy One. *Thrill of the Chase Blog.* Retrieved from https://dalneitzel.com/2017/04/04/scrapbook-one-hundred-seventy-one/

58. Fenn, F. (2017, April 5). Scrapbook One Hundred Seventy Two. *Thrill of the Chase Blog.* Retrieved from https://dalneitzel.com/2017/04/05/scrapbook-one-hundred-seventy-two/

59. Fenn, F. (2017, April 7). Scrapbook One Hundred Seventy Three. *Thrill of the Chase Blog.* Retrieved from https://dalneitzel.com/2017/04/07/scrapbook-one-hundred-seventy-three/

60. Fenn, F. (2017, April 8). Scrapbook One Hundred Seventy Four. *Thrill of the Chase Blog*. Retrieved from https://dalneitzel.com/2017/04/08/scrapbook-one-hundred-seventy-four/

61. Fenn, F. (2017, April 10). Scrapbook One Hundred Seventy Five. *Thrill of the Chase Blog*. Retrieved from https://dalneitzel.com/2017/04/10/scrapbook-one-hundred-seventy-five/

62. Fenn, F. (2017, April 12). Scrapbook One Hundred Seventy Seven. *Thrill of the Chase Blog*. Retrieved from https://dalneitzel.com/2017/04/12/scrapbook-one-hundred-seventy-seven/

63. Fenn, F. (2017, April 17). Scrapbook One Hundred Eighty. *Thrill of the Chase Blog*. Retrieved from https://dalneitzel.com/2017/04/17/scrapbook-one-hundred-eighty/

64. Fenn, F. (2017, April 21). Scrapbook One Hundred Eighty One. *Thrill of the Chase Blog*. Retrieved from https://dalneitzel.com/2017/04/21/scrapbook-one-hundred-eighty-one/

65. Fenn, F. (2017, April 24). Scrapbook One Hundred Eighty Two. *Thrill of the Chase Blog*. Retrieved from https://dalneitzel.com/2017/04/24/scrapbook-one-hundred-eighty-two/

66. Fenn, F. (2017, November 22). Scrapbook One Hundred Eighty Five. *Thrill of the Chase Blog*. Retrieved from https://dalneitzel.com/2017/11/22/scrapbook-one-hundred-eighty-five/

67. Fenn, F. (2018, June 21). Scrapbook One Hundred Eighty Eight. *Thrill of the Chase Blog*. Retrieved

from https://dalneitzel.com/2018/06/21/scrapbook-one-hundred-eighty-eight/

68. Fenn, F. (2018, September 26). Scrapbook One Hundred Ninety. *Thrill of the Chase Blog*. Retrieved from https://dalneitzel.com/2018/09/26/scrapbook-one-hundred-ninety/

69. Fenn, F. (2018, September 30). Scrapbook One Hundred Ninety One. *Thrill of the Chase Blog*. Retrieved from https://dalneitzel.com/2018/09/30/scrapbook-one-hundred-ninetyone/

70. Fenn, F. (2019, March 11). Scrapbook One Hundred Ninety Eight. *Thrill of the Chase Blog*. Retrieved from https://dalneitzel.com/2019/03/11/scrapbook-one-hundred-ninety-eight/

71. Fenn, F. (2019, April 15). Scrapbook One Hundred Ninety Nine *Thrill of the Chase Blog*. Retrieved from https://dalneitzel.com/2019/04/15/scrapbook-one-hundred-ninety-nine/

72. Fenn, F. (2019, May 20). Scrapbook Two Hundred One. *Thrill of the Chase Blog*. Retrieved from https://dalneitzel.com/2019/05/20/scrapbook-two_hundred-one/

73. Fenn, F. (2019, June 14). Scrapbook Two Hundred Two. *Thrill of the Chase Blog*. Retrieved from https://dalneitzel.com/2019/06/14/scrapbook-two_hundred-two/

74. Fenn, F. (2019, August 15). Scrapbook Two Hundred Three. *Thrill of the Chase Blog*. Retrieved from https://dalneitzel.com/2019/08/15/scrapbook-two_hundred-three/

75. Fenn, F. (2019, August 16). Scrapbook Two Hundred Four. *Thrill of the Chase Blog*. Retrieved from https://daln-

eitzel.com/2019/08/16/scrapbook-two_hundred-four/

76. Fenn, F. (2019, September 15). Scrapbook Two Hundred Five. *Thrill of the Chase Blog*. Retrieved from https://dalneitzel.com/2019/09/15/scrapbook-two_hundred-five/

77. Fenn, F. (2019, September 30). Scrapbook Two Hundred Eight. *Thrill of the Chase Blog*. Retrieved from https://dalneitzel.com/2019/09/30/scrapbook-two_hundred-eight/

78. Fenn, F. (2019, October 4). Scrapbook Two Hundred Nine. *Thrill of the Chase Blog*. Retrieved from https://dalneitzel.com/2019/10/04/scrapbook-two_hundred-nine/

79. Fenn, F. (2019, October 9). Scrapbook Two Hundred Ten. *Thrill of the Chase Blog*. Retrieved from https://dalneitzel.com/2019/10/09/scrapbook-two_hundred-ten/

80. Fenn, F. (2019, October 10). Scrapbook Two Hundred Eleven. *Thrill of the Chase Blog*. Retrieved from https://dalneitzel.com/2019/10/10/scrapbook-two_hundred-eleven/

81. Fenn, F. (2019, October 12). Scrapbook Two Hundred Twelve. *Thrill of the Chase Blog*. Retrieved from https://dalneitzel.com/2019/10/12/scrapbook-two_hundred-twelve/

82. Fenn, F. (2019, October 13). Scrapbook Two Hundred Thirteen. *Thrill of the Chase Blog*. Retrieved from https://dalneitzel.com/2019/10/13/scrapbook-two_hundred-thirteen/

83. Fenn, F. (2019, October 16). Scrapbook Two Hundred Fourteen. *Thrill of the Chase Blog*. Retrieved from https://dalneitzel.com/2019/10/16/scrapbook-two_hun-

dred-fourteen/

84. Fenn, F. (2019, October 20). Scrapbook Two Hundred Fifteen. *Thrill of the Chase Blog.* Retrieved from https://dalneitzel.com/2019/10/20/scrapbook-two_hundred-fifteen/

85. Fenn, F. (2019, October 22). Scrapbook Two Hundred Sixteen. *Thrill of the Chase Blog.* Retrieved from https://dalneitzel.com/2019/10/22/scrapbook-two_hundred-sixteen/

86. Fenn, F. (2019, October 23). Scrapbook Two Hundred Seventeen. *Thrill of the Chase Blog.* Retrieved from https://dalneitzel.com/2019/10/23/scrapbook-two_hundred-seventeen/

87. Fenn, F. (2019, October 26). Scrapbook Two Hundred Nineteen. *Thrill of the Chase Blog.* Retrieved from https://dalneitzel.com/2019/10/26/scrapbook-two_hundred-nineteeen/

88. Fenn, F. (2019, October 27). Scrapbook Two Hundred Twenty. *Thrill of the Chase Blog.* Retrieved from https://dalneitzel.com/2019/10/27/scrapbook-two_hundred-twenty/

89. Fenn, F. (2019, October 28). Scrapbook Two Hundred Twenty One. *Thrill of the Chase Blog.* Retrieved from https://dalneitzel.com/2019/10/28/scrapbook-two_hundred-twenty-one/

90. Fenn, F. (2019, October 30). Scrapbook Two Hundred Twenty Two. *Thrill of the Chase Blog.* Retrieved from https://dalneitzel.com/2019/10/30/scrapbook-two_hundred-twenty-two/

91. Fenn, F. (2019, October 31). Scrapbook Two Hundred Twenty Three. *Thrill of the Chase Blog*. Retrieved from https://dalneitzel.com/2019/10/31/scrapbook-two_hundred-twenty-three-2/

92. Fenn, F. (2019, November 1). Scrapbook Two Hundred Twenty Four. *Thrill of the Chase Blog*. Retrieved from https://dalneitzel.com/2019/11/01/scrapbook-two_hundred-twenty-four/

93. Fenn, F. (2019, November 2). Scrapbook Two Hundred Twenty Five. *Thrill of the Chase Blog*. Retrieved from https://dalneitzel.com/2019/11/02/scrapbook-two_hundred-twenty-five/

94. Fenn, F. (2019, November 3). Scrapbook Two Hundred Twenty Six. *Thrill of the Chase Blog*. Retrieved from https://dalneitzel.com/2019/11/03/scrapbook-two_hundred-twenty-six/

95. Fenn, F. (2019, November 5). Scrapbook Two Hundred Twenty Seven. *Thrill of the Chase Blog*. Retrieved from https://dalneitzel.com/2019/11/05/scrapbook-two_hundred-twenty-seven/

96. Fenn, F. (2019, November 7). Scrapbook Two Hundred Twenty Eight. *Thrill of the Chase Blog*. Retrieved from https://dalneitzel.com/2019/11/07/scrapbook-two_hundred-twenty-eight/

97. Fenn, F. (2019, November 10). Scrapbook Two Hundred Twenty Nine. *Thrill of the Chase Blog*. Retrieved from https://dalneitzel.com/2019/11/10/scrapbook-two_hundred-twenty-nine/

98. Fenn, F. (2019, November 11). Scrapbook Two Hundred

Thirty. *Thrill of the Chase Blog.* Retrieved from https://dalneitzel.com/2019/11/11/scrapbook-two_hundred-thirty/

99. Fenn, F. (2019, November 13). Scrapbook Two Hundred Thirty One. *Thrill of the Chase Blog.* Retrieved from https://dalneitzel.com/2019/11/13/scrapbook-two_hundred-thirty-one/

100. Fenn, F. (2019, November 14). Scrapbook Two Hundred Thirty Two. *Thrill of the Chase Blog.* Retrieved from https://dalneitzel.com/2019/11/14/scrapbook-two_hundred-thirty-two/

101. Fenn, F. (2019, November 15). Scrapbook Two Hundred Thirty Three. *Thrill of the Chase Blog.* Retrieved from https://dalneitzel.com/2019/11/15/scrapbook-two_hundred-thirty-three/

102. Fenn, F. (2019, November 16). Scrapbook Two Hundred Thirty Four. *Thrill of the Chase Blog.* Retrieved from https://dalneitzel.com/2019/11/16/scrapbook-two_hundred-thirty-four/

103. Fenn, F. (2019, November 17). Scrapbook Two Hundred Thirty Five. *Thrill of the Chase Blog.* Retrieved from https://dalneitzel.com/2019/11/17/scrapbook-two_hundred-thirty-five/

104. Fenn, F. (2019, November 18). Scrapbook Two Hundred Thirty Six. *Thrill of the Chase Blog.* Retrieved from https://dalneitzel.com/2019/11/18/scrapbook-two_hundred-thirty-six/

105. Fenn, F. (2019, November 21). Scrapbook Two Hundred Thirty Eight. *Thrill of the Chase Blog.* Retrieved from https://dalneitzel.com/2019/11/21/scrap-

book-two_hundred-thirty-eight/

106. Fenn, F. (2019, November 23). Scrapbook Two Hundred Forty. *Thrill of the Chase Blog*. Retrieved from https://dalneitzel.com/2019/11/23/scrapbook-two_hundred-thirty-forty/

107. Fenn, F. (2019, November 24). Scrapbook Two Hundred Forty One. *Thrill of the Chase Blog*. Retrieved from https://dalneitzel.com/2019/11/24/scrapbook-two_hundred-forty-one/

108. Fenn, F. (2019, November 27). Scrapbook Two Hundred Forty Two. *Thrill of the Chase Blog*. Retrieved from https://dalneitzel.com/2019/11/27/scrapbook-two_hundred-forty-two/

109. Fenn, F. (2019, November 29). Scrapbook Two Hundred Forty Three. *Thrill of the Chase Blog*. Retrieved from https://dalneitzel.com/2019/11/29/scrapbook-two_hundred-forty-three/

110. Fenn, F. (2019, December 7). Scrapbook Two Hundred Forty Four. *Thrill of the Chase Blog*. Retrieved from https://dalneitzel.com/2019/12/07/scrapbook-two_hundred-forty-four/

111. Fenn, F. (2019, December 8). Scrapbook Two Hundred Forty Five. *Thrill of the Chase Blog*. Retrieved from https://dalneitzel.com/2019/12/08/scrapbook-two_hundred-forty-five/

112. Fenn, F. (2019, December 12). Scrapbook Two Hundred Forty Seven. *Thrill of the Chase Blog*. Retrieved from https://dalneitzel.com/2019/12/12/scrapbook-two_hundred-forty-seven/

113. Fenn, F. (2020, January 24). Scrapbook Two Hundred Forty Eight. *Thrill of the Chase Blog.* Retrieved from https://dalneitzel.com/2020/01/24/scrapbook-two_hundred-forty-eight/

114. Fenn, F. (2020, March 18). Scrapbook Two Hundred Forty Nine. *Thrill of the Chase Blog.* Retrieved from https://dalneitzel.com/2020/03/18/scrapbook-two_hundred-forty-nine/

115. Fenn, F. (2020, April 9). Scrapbook Two Hundred Fifty Two. *Thrill of the Chase Blog.* Retrieved from https://dalneitzel.com/2020/04/09/scrapbook-two_hundred-fifty-two/

116. *New International Version.* Bible Gateway. Web. Retrieved on 20 February 2020.

117. Brown, A. (2016). *The Oracle: Universal Law of Prosperity.* Bloomington, IN: WestBow Press.

ABOUT THE AUTHOR

Aaron Brown

Aaron Brown enjoys penning his thoughts in hopes of inspiring readers to pursue an enlightened path with purpose. An alumnus of Moody Bible Institute in Chicago and graduate of Texas A&M University, Aaron is author of THE ORACLE: Universal Law of Prosperity Defying All Others, and co-founder of an eclectic cafe named Sweet Eugene's. He lives in Texas with  his charming wife and two adorable daughters.

BOOKS BY THIS AUTHOR

The Oracle: Universal Law Of Prosperity Defying All Others

The Oracle is the enlightenment of a profound principle the author learned during a desperate season of his life. The power to transform a life finally awakened him. Embracing its message on one of his darkest days, he wrote The Oracle to revive hope and inspiration for the prosperity God offers each of us.

The Oracle assures the favor of God to the soul who observes its message, and a curse to the one who rejects it. Promoting a shift in one's mind, this universal law prompts wellness, abundance, hope, purpose, and a radically enriched life destiny.

Ensuring the transformation of life and soul, The Oracle boasts promises almost too good to be true. Almost.

Made in the USA
Columbia, SC
23 July 2023

20769998R00080